CASE STUDIES IN CULTURAL ANTHROPOLOGY

SERIES EDITORS

George and Louise Spindler

STANFORD UNIVERSITY

THE WHITE MAN WILL EAT YOU!

An Anthropologist among the Imbonggu of New Guinea

THE WHITE MAN WILL EAT YOU!

An Anthropologist among the Imbonggu of New Guinea

WILLIAM E. WORMSLEY

Emory University
and
Georgia State University

Harcourt Brace Jovanovich College Publishers

FORT WORTH PHILADELPHIA SAN DIEGO NEW YORK
ORLANDO AUSTIN SAN ANTONIO
TORONTO MONTREAL LONDON SYDNEY TOKYO

To my wife Diane

and my son Patai

Also to my parents, Orley and Louise Wormsley,

and my parents-in-law, Carl and Lona Pomeroy

Editor in Chief Ted Buchholz
Acquisitions Editor Christopher P. Klein
Senior Project Editor Kay Kaylor
Production Manager Debra A. Jenkin
Designer Sok James Hwang

ISBN: 0-15-500196-5

Library of Congress Catalog Number: 92-81264

Printed in the United States of America

2 3 4 5 6 7 8 9 0 016 9 8 7 6 5 4 3 2 1

Foreword

ABOUT THE SERIES

These case studies in cultural anthropology are designed to bring students in beginning and intermediate courses in the social sciences insights into the richness and complexity of human life as it is lived in various ways in different places. The authors are men and women who have lived in the societies they write about and who are professionally trained as observers and interpreters of human behavior. In addition, the authors are teachers; in their writings, the needs of the student reader remain foremost. We, the editors, believe that by understanding ways of life very different from our own, abstractions and generalizations about the human condition become meaningful.

The scope and character of the series has changed since we published the first case studies in 1960. This is in keeping with our intention to represent anthropology as it is. We are concerned with the ways in which human groups and communities are coping with the massive changes wrought in their physical and sociopolitical environments in recent decades. We are also concerned with the ways in which established cultures have solved life's problems. And we want to represent the various modes of communication and emphasis that are being formed and reformed as anthropology itself changes.

We think of this as an instructional series, intended for use in the classroom. We have always used case studies in our teaching, whether for beginning students or advanced graduate students. We start with case studies, whether from our own series or from elsewhere, and weave our way into theory, and then turn again to cases. For us, they are the foundation of our discipline.

ABOUT THE AUTHOR

William E. Wormsley, born in 1945, spent the bulk of his youth in Unadilla, a small town in upstate New York. He began his undergraduate career in 1964 at Harpur College (State University of New York at Binghamton). In 1966, as American involvement in Vietnam grew, he was drafted and served two years in the U.S. Army. His final ten months of duty were spent in Quang Tri Province, immediately south of what then was the DMZ (demilitarized zone) between North and South Vietnam. It was that experience, his first outside the United States, that led him to enroll in his first anthropology course. Upon his return to America, he enrolled at State University of New York at Brockport to complete his final two years of undergraduate study. He completed his B.A. in 1970. In 1971, he was offered a graduate teaching assistantship to attend the University of Pittsburgh and pursue a doctorate in anthropology. After more than two years of research among the Imbonggu in New Guinea, he was awarded a Ph.D. in 1978. After appointments at the University of Kansas and Illinois State University, he returned to Papua New Guinea in January 1981 as a Research Fellow at the Institute of Applied Social and Economic Research, where he developed a research program centered on tribal violence in the highlands provinces. In March 1982, he was appointed to the post of Social Anthropologist with the Papua New Guinea Public Services Commission. For the next three and one-half years, he was a team member of a World Bank rural development program. His research focused on the issue of tribal warfare among the Enga. In 1985, he returned to America as Visiting Assistant Professor of Anthropology at the University of Iowa for one year before accepting a permanent position at the University of Wyoming in 1986. During the next three years, he made two research trips to Yap, in Western Micronesia, to study the use and abuse of alcohol. In 1989, he was awarded a Fulbright Scholar Award, which sent him to Bangkok, Thailand, for a year (1989–90). He taught anthropology at Silpakorn University and conducted research on the issue of AIDS, prostitution, and tourism. After devoting eighteen months to writing, Wormsley made a long-overdue return trip to Vietnam in 1992. He is currently completing a book based on his Fulbright year in Thailand to be followed by a book based on his experiences in Vietnam (1968 and 1992).

ABOUT THIS CASE STUDY

This case study represents anthropology as a cultural critique and as reflexive anthropology. It is more than "straight" ethnography but provides as well most of what any good conventional ethnography could. The interaction between the author-anthropologist and the Imbonggu is a constant thread that ties the narrative together. We come to know both in a way that is quite different than when the anthropologist is merely an observer and the "natives" are the observed. Both the anthropologist and the natives become humanized and therefore become understandable. "Billio" (William Wormsley) is not just an observer, or just a participant, in the usual sense. He becomes a special person to the Imbonggu, with a special status and known idiosyncracies. He is his own agent in disputes; he is a myth- and storyteller (but not a terribly good one because his stock of myths and stories from his own culture is meager); he is a friend; he is a potential mate, from the Imbonggu point of view; he is a source of cigarettes, aspirin, and limited medical aid; and he is an informant about a world the Imbonggu are just beginning to encounter and wonder about. Visits to his house are interesting, and both men and women come there to spend hours in conversation. He intersects with a wide variety of people. One has the sense that few of them are inaccessible to him, irrespective of gender, age, or position.

As readers of *The White Man Will Eat You!* we are caught up in the narrative. We learn about the anthropologist-informant interaction, about how the anthropologist felt, and what he thought, as he experienced life in a community so distant from his home in miles and culture. We also learn about the Imbonggu. We are introduced to social structure, subsistence techniques, social and economic exchange and obligations, bridewealth, political process, leadership, religion and magic—the conventional rubrics of inclusive ethnography—and to the theory that guides their interpretation. But we learn about these matters as though we were companions of the anthropologist, there in person among the Imbonggu.

When the time comes to leave the place and people we have come to know with Billio, we leave with regret and face, as he did, the inhumanity of our own culture. The critique of that culture, delivered in the last chapters, is a classic statement. It will irritate some readers, as it did one of the students who wrote on his evaluation of a class taught by Professor Wormsley that if the latter liked it so much among the Imbonggu he should return to New Guinea and live like a savage! Many anthropologists will recognize their own feelings in Wormsley's words. Culture shock for many of us is something we experience on coming home.

This case study should be of value to students in introductory courses who want to know about anthropologists as well as the cultures they study. It should also be of value to anyone who wants to gain perspective on humanity and on human behavior. We will make it required reading for our courses in both multicultural education and basic anthropology.

GEORGE and LOUISE SPINDLER
Series Editors
Ethnographics
P.O. Box 38
Calistoga, CA 94515

SUGGESTED FILMS

First Contact. Australian Broadcastng Commission, 1983. This film presents the experience of initial contact between three Australian gold prospectors and various peoples of the interior of New Guinea. It tells the story from both perspectives. The film's existence is attributable to the fortuitous discovery of original black-and-white film footage uncatalogued in a film archive in Australia. That film was shot by one of the gold prospectors (Mick Leahy) in the early 1930s. *First Contact* is constructed around that original footage plus contemporary footage of interviews with various surviving parties to the events of that initial period of cultural contact. The film runs approximately fifty-five minutes.

The Kawelka: Ongka's Big Moka. Granada Television International, 1974. This film is one of several titles in The Disappearing World Series. Set in the Western Highlands of Papua New Guinea, it focuses on the activities of a particular Big Man among the Kawelka people. Ongka, the Big Man, seeks to amass the most impressive public gift of pigs in the annals of the Kawelka. The film traces his steps as he negotiates with other Big Men to set the stage for his enormous public gift, which ultimately includes hundreds of pigs, thousands of dollars' worth of currency, and a Toyota Land Cruiser truck. This gift, when given to Ongka's chief competitor, established Ongka's reputation as a Big Man for the ages. The film runs fifty-two minutes.

Acknowledgments

Field research among the Imbonggu between May 1975 and August 1977 was made possible by a doctoral dissertation grant from the National Science Foundation. The Department of Anthropology, University of Pittsburgh, provided a small supplementary grant. I thank both institutions for their financial support. My debt to each is far greater than the dollar amounts provided. I am further indebted to the Department of Anthropology, University of Pittsburgh, and several key faculty members without whose confidence and support I would have been unable to benefit from my extended association with the Imbonggu. In particular, I wish to thank Alexander Spoehr, chairman of my dissertation committee. It is impossible to express the depth of my admiration for him, both as an anthropologist and as an individual. He and his wife Anne have continued to provide support and encouragement through the years. As members of my dissertation committee, Keith Brown, John Singleton, and Christina Bratt Paulston each contributed significantly to my research.

Since completing the research described here, I have benefited from enlightening discussions with several people concerning the nature of anthropological fieldwork and the various forms in which anthropologists present it. For such discussion and advice I wish to offer thanks to June Helm and Mac Marshall, University of Iowa; Akira Yamamoto, Kimiko Yamamoto, Allan Hanson, and Louise Hanson, University of Kansas; Rob Dirks, Illinois State University; Audrey Shalinsky and Don Frazier, University of Wyoming; and Srisakra Vallibhotama, Chinan Wongvipak, and Rasmi Shoocongdej, Silpakorn University, Bangkok, Thailand. Three individuals did much to encourage the present enterprise while I was resident in Bangkok (1989–90) as a Fulbright Scholar and a fellow of Thailand's John F. Kennedy Foundation. Bert Elishewitz, Maria Elishewitz, and Doris Wibunsin urged me to write this account but to do so in a way that would make the content appealing to those who are not professional anthropologists. I hope they will approve of this effort.

In Australia and New Guinea, Peter Lawrence was a constant source of support and friendship both during the period of field research in Ialibu and later in Enga. In New Guinea, my debts mounted quickly. Among the non-Imbonggu community of Ialibu, Southern Highlands, I wish to express gratitude to Geoff and Anne Cowper, Dennis and Edith Elder, Bob and Sandy Vogel, Gavin and Kay Spillane, John Brady, Bob Saunders, John Koma, John Jones, Sarah Livingston, Max Briggs, Mark Rosen, Jack Bullock, Dave Ekins, and Raphael Tolnga. My deepest gratitude goes to Randy Bollig. He provided a roof and a bed when I visited the Ialibu government station and has remained a very close friend.

But my greatest appreciation is reserved for the people of Ialibu, particularly those with whom I lived for more than two years in the village of Tona. Without specifying the nature of individual contributions, I express my love and appreciation to everyone in Tona. Special mention is due Yoke, Agaiye, Garu, Temane, Daga, Yombi, Tope, Lyawa, Eiea, Vincent, Tendako, Napile, Mopune, Mone, Kupini, Poyome, Simon, Nasinolo, Ulli, and Wane. I only regret that I cannot name everyone. I apologize to those who may be disappointed by my use of pseudonyms in the book itself.

Finally, during the actual writing of the book I have benefited from the encouraging comments of several individuals who have read the entire manuscript or portions of it. Such thanks go to Mac Marshall, George Spindler, Gardner Spungin, Kay Kaylor, and Diane Wormsley. The latter, my wife, has done much more than merely read the manuscript. She has been both source of support and model of tolerance for my extensive (and probably compulsive) anthropological wanderings. I can think of no adequate acknowledgment for her contribution. My six-year-old son Patai displayed an uncommon willingness to excuse me from my designated role as Luigi—he is invariably Mario—for extended periods of time while I played with words instead of with him.

While all those who have contributed to this enterprise in one way or another are deserving of credit for whatever success it ultimately enjoys, none save me is responsible for its shortcomings. They are my contribution, and mine alone.

Contents

Illustrations

Map

Photographs

1 / If You Had a Mind, You'd Be out of It

On May 5, 1975, I arrived in New Guinea to begin a two-year anthropological study (Wormsley 1978). I was ready. My graduate committee at the University of Pittsburgh had written letters on my behalf and established an enviable network which would guarantee my personal and professional survival in New Guinea. The trip to New Guinea was leisurely with stops in Honolulu, Suva (Fiji), Brisbane, Canberra, and Sydney. As if to test my preparedness, Qantas, the Australian airline, was humbled by the traditional labor strike. As a result, I arrived in New Guinea three months behind schedule.

Professor Spoehr, my doctoral advisor, had prepared me for every conceivable medical situation. I knew of chloroquine, Lomotil, and a dozen other remedies. On May 9, my third day in New Guinea, my mind raced through them in an effort to determine which would allow me to save face, or lose the least of it, on an equatorially hot and humid day in Lea Lea, a beautiful little village near Papua New Guinea's national capital, Port Moresby. I was included in a party of foreign guests invited to visit Lea Lea for the day. Part of the program was a meal. My first New Guinean meal. I anticipated fish, maybe some pig, probably some yams and taro.

They were all there, but as side dishes to the main courses. The main courses were not the first foods ever to appear to return my stare. In Brisbane, Australia, only three months earlier I had ordered my first filet of sole. It was my first intact anything. Its lifeless left eye never once blinked nor even momentarily forfeited my gaze. It hadn't been easy, but my hunger had overcome my unease. It may have been unappealing, but it was only a fish, after all.

That had been Brisbane. The plattered menagerie returning my stare in Lea Lea also contained fish, but it was encircled by some truly astonishing companions. The duck was charred black, its identity thus totally obscured. The small intact crocodile tasted reasonably like chicken. Hardly a recommendation, of course, given the American tendency to describe all indescribable foods as tasting like chicken. But the pièce de résistance was certainly the wallaby. It was also complete, including long tail. Its face was contorted, its skin drawn into a hideous smile. Turning a large, not overly intelligent cow into steaks seems acceptable, possibly even appropriate, but, in contrast, small, cute animals deserve cuddling and protection. This would not be easy. Looking back, I cannot recall the taste of the bird or the wallaby. No hints of their taste or texture appear in my field notes for that day. I assume my mind was on other things. But the day served as an omen of meals to come.

From Lea Lea, I returned to my room at the Waigani Lodge. The Australian National University had for many years operated a research center in Port Moresby. Known as the New Guinea Research Unit, it was a mecca for foreign researchers, especially anthropologists. The Research Unit contained, among other things, an excellent library and a comfortable guest lodge. As I lay in my bed at the lodge, I found myself reflecting on the day's meal, as well as numerous conversations with family and friends prior to my departure for New Guinea. To a person, they had doubted my sanity. New Guinea was either at the end of the earth or slightly beyond there. It was dirty, hot, humid, insect ridden, disease infested, and populated by unpleasant people. My parents, relatives, and friends had all seen unflattering television documentaries or read the sensational accounts of the *National Geographic*. There was also the legacy of Michael Rockefeller's mysterious disappearance. Their predictions for my future and survival were as ugly as their understanding of New Guinea and its people. I would probably die, or at least become incurably ill with some tropical disease. And should I survive the dangers of the place, there still remained the people. Not just people, I was reminded, but cannibals. Probably the same cannibals who had eaten the unfortunate Rockefeller.

Was I really up to this? There were many reasons to doubt my readiness. Diane, my wife, was teaching in Brisbane, Australia, in preference to accompanying me to New Guinea. Her reasons were professional. She was pursuing her own career, and a lengthy time-out from it seemed to carry risks. She would be teaching at the Narbethong School for Visually Handicapped Children. Brisbane seemed close enough to New Guinea. We had made plans for me to travel to Brisbane during Christmas holiday breaks in 1975 and 1976. Diane would visit me in New Guinea in May and August 1976 while on her school holidays. During those first few weeks in New Guinea, she seemed further away than Brisbane. So far away, in fact, that I made an unscheduled trip to Brisbane for a week in September.

While sitting out the Qantas strike, and again during my unscheduled field break visiting Diane, I made a great many new friends in Brisbane. Most of them presented the same dismal picture of New Guinea as that held by friends and relatives back in the United States. But by September 1975 I was suspecting that all those uninformed detractors were wrong. By August 1977, I knew it. That learning process, over nearly two and one-half years, was an incredible roller coaster-like trip. There were exhilarating highs and unfathomable lows. Both contributed to what I continue to regard as the most exciting period of my life. I learned much about myself and much about "cannibals." I discovered uncounted ways in which we differed, and those differences fascinated me. They continue to fascinate me. More amazing were the uncounted ways in which we were alike. Those similarities continue to fascinate me as well.

My journey to understanding the Imbonggu (they were my cannibals) and myself (I was theirs) is the subject of this book. Retelling the incidents contained in this book isn't really like reliving them. It is more as if I never left. In many ways I did not leave. Spontaneous eruptions of Imbonggu gestures, sounds, and words mark the continuing link. Even more telling are the Imbonggu interpretations of American events. They are not contrived, they are now and forever expressions of a part of me. On those rare occasions when I receive letters from Imbonggu friends, I find myself actually hearing the speech more than reading it. Sadly, time has begun to erode that process of communication, and letters no longer arrive from Imbonggu, although one particularly close Enga friend continues to write faithfully. This book is in some ways an attempt to recover something which is on the verge of becoming lost. With this book, I am back in my grass hut in Tona. I am with some of my best friends and some of my worst. Introducing them is my pleasure. I hope it will prove to be yours as well.

2 / Culture Shock

Culture shock is one of the staples of anthropology. For those who wish to understand why humans do what they do in the various ways in which they do it, culture shock is an occupational hazard which triggers profound responses in the anthropologist, both as scientist and as human.

What has always been the source of bonding in the community of professional anthropologists has become chic, however. In that process of diffusion to the general populace, the concept has become trivialized. Tourists return from exotic travels with tales of their bouts with "culture shock," usually laced with unrecognized doses of ethnocentrism. This is an affliction also well known to anthropologists, although we hope not from our personal worldview. Ethnocentrism paralyzes the intellect so as to facilitate, or at least permit, the view that whatever *we* have or do is better than what *they* have or do.

In most cases, the demonstration of one's ethnocentric proclivities serves primarily to mark one as an outsider. The politically appealing judgment that America is quite simply the "greatest" or "best" or "most free" nation in the world is noncontroversial when the audience is dominated by Americans who are all equally convinced of the truth of the assertion. The same proclamations are greeted with skepticism, and often with anger, when uttered by Americans in the heart of London, Stockholm, or Bangkok. Little is lost, or gained, if the result is no more than the rebuttal judgments that Americans are uninformed, condescending, crude in manner, and self-centered. Americans merely demonstrate their role as outsiders.

However, occasions arise, and they have been numerous throughout history, when ethnocentrism approximates some form of terminal mental illness. For instance, during the American involvement in Vietnam in the 1960s and 1970s, it was common to hear judgments concerning the politically repressive, morally corrupt, and militarily incompetent communist government of North Vietnam. While such views were politically appealing to the patriotic, they were sadly inaccurate. The result was a military defeat (which proved to be less humbling than it should have been), one in which much of the world revelled. After all, one of the wonderfully appropriate punishments of ethnocentrism is the inevitable meal of "crow" that follows indulgence. Following World War II, Japanese-manufactured products held the American reputation of junk. Forty years later, American products have usurped that designation, even among Americans.

Ethnocentrism thrives best in those who combine ignorance of the culture they are evaluating with ignorance of their own. Thus tourist friends bore us with esoteric accounts of trains that run late, food that forces them to look forward to a return to McDonald's, tour guides and merchants who speak flawed English, entire nations that lack twenty-four-hour television, streets populated by pickpockets and prostitutes, and "funny money" that comes in various shapes, sizes, and colors. Clearly, most of the world has a great deal to learn.

As an anthropologist, I am seldom more bored than when listening to such tales, for they hardly ever offer insight into the lives and values of the people being described. What I learn about Thailand or Papua New Guinea is trivial. Papua New Guinea has no good hotels. Thai food is too spicy because the heat overwhelms any flavors that might be present. I heard both these judgments in Laramie, Wyoming, a delightful town but one known neither for its hotels nor its cuisine. Those same tales, ostensibly about somewhere else, are most instructive for what they communicate about Americans, or their western European cousins generally. And, sadly, they communicate a great deal.

What they convey most eloquently, without demanding detailed analysis, is the extent of our ignorance of the culture with which we feel most comfortable—our own. That someone else's planes are always late is a curious judgment from someone living in a society that considers airlines "on time" if they take off or arrive within fifteen minutes of published times. Short-hop commuter passengers could spend nearly as much time on the ground being "on time" as on the plane in flight! Americans' self-righteous complaints that there are prostitutes everywhere in Manila and Bangkok sound humorous when we consider almost any urban center of a million people in America. Thais offended with their Patpong would be justly horrified at what occurs on 42nd Street in New York or Sunset Strip in Los Angeles. One evening in Thailand I met a young man from San Francisco who suggested that Bangkok should change its name, given the city's image as a center of sex and sin. He seemed unaware that the name "Bangkok" is the product of earlier foreigners like himself who were unable to pronounce the name "Bang Makok." He seemed to sense no irony in the nightly meanderings of leggy prostitutes through San Francisco's "Tenderloin" in evening wear from Frederick's of Hollywood.

Culture shock, as perceived by tourists and other transients, is trivialized because it adds nothing to our understanding of humanity, of which those transients are a part. What might have become a satisfying intellectual voyage of discovery stagnates in a quagmire of misunderstanding and ignorance. Ignorance of someone else, and ignorance of themselves. While tourists think of culture shock as a hurdle to be overcome, anthropologists usually think of it as a sign of the presence of something worth investigating.

The essence of anthropological inquiry is the desire to go beyond superficial understanding. We do that by immersing ourselves in a different cultural and social system. It is not enough to venture out of the Hilton for a few hours to haggle with an illiterate gem dealer. We demand of ourselves that we do more than learn a few phrases that will produce the foods to which we are accustomed. Anthropologists demand of one another that we immerse ourselves as deeply as possible in our adopted societies. Few tourists, no matter how travelworn their backpacks, make such an investment. But the investment pays considerable dividends in expanded understanding. As an anthropologist, I know another culture or society as more than a mere collection of interesting or not-so-interesting facts. I know a culture as a system of beliefs, values, and institutions by which the members of that society conceptualize, create, and manipulate those facts, both interesting and not-so-interesting. In other words, I know the logic of a culture. I can explain past and current events and predict responses with reasonable accuracy.

On the one hand, this understanding is exhilarating. Ignorance has been replaced by knowledge. It is profoundly satisfying. However, at the same time, it is frequently disturbing. It often leads the anthropologist back into culture shock in a way that tourists, businesspeople, missionaries, and government officers almost never experience. A congregation of anthropologists is a fascinating gathering for the uninitiated. One evening at a party, I found myself conversing with the nonanthropologist escort of one of my anthropologist friends. He was seeing his companion's professional world for the first time. He talked at some length about the obvious role of fieldwork as a bonding agent among anthropologists. He was positively impressed at the manner in which fieldwork provided a seemingly endless pool of "war stories."

He was less favorably impressed by what he saw as an extreme tendency toward criticizing American culture and society. I explained to him that what he had detected was culture shock as it is most often experienced by anthropologists. Unlike transient visitors, anthropologists seldom return home to resume their lives with little more than a few exciting stories and exotic trinkets to be shared with envious friends and neighbors. Anthropologists return with heads, notebooks, tapes, and photographs full of beliefs, knowledge, and values that are different but no longer new and unfamiliar. Now home is new and unfamiliar and it demands the effort at understanding. Every anthropologist I know finds returning home to be more stressful than going to the field. And many find that returning home is never completely satisfying. As James Peoples and Garrick Bailey note, "deep immersion into other sociocultural systems leaves some of us unsure about our attachment to our own" (1988:435).

Returning to the cocktail conversation alluded to above, my nonanthropologist observer nodded vigorously, exclaiming that he had never considered the possibility of "reverse culture shock." Not wishing to deliver a lecture, I nevertheless felt the urge to redefine what I feared was his inaccurate understanding. To describe the phenomenon as "reverse" seemed to imply a degree of directionality that I feel is misleading and dangerous. Reverse has meaning only with reference to forward. And, of course, forward is positive while reverse is negative. By extension, he seemed to be saying that culture shock is natural in one direction and not in the other. In other words, some cultures are more shocking than others. I prefer to think of culture shock as something that occurs at the juncture of cultural systems where understanding is the goal. What tourists experience is seldom culture shock at all, precisely because no sense of cultural values is sought or achieved. What tourists feel is rarely more than homesickness. While it may be more or less acute depending on their threshold for discomfort, what tourists experience is seldom the product of an intellectual attempt to rationalize competing systems of thought, neither or none of which is fully comprehended.

I noted earlier that culture shock is an occupational hazard for anthropologists. It is more profoundly a hazard than those encountered by other social scientists, however. One of my professors in graduate school once told me that anthropology, if done properly, is not a profession; it is a way of life. Anthropologists seek to understand human behavior and social institutions in a truly comprehensive manner. As a result, we are constantly observing people and what they do. Unlike our fellows in society, we are seldom content to accept behavior on faith as "normal" or "traditional" or "customary" or "good" or "proper." To do so places us at risk of illustrating the evils of ethnocentrism and ignorance of the meaning and consequences of our own actions. The anthropologist's inability to partake of culture without attempting to achieve understanding produces a fascinating irony. We find that what most Americans know least is what we know best. And what we should understand best, if for no other reason than our native membership in it, is our own culture. But, of course, that is the one we understand least.

Sadly, we are in good company in the numerical sense that most Americans know far less about their society and culture than they think they do. For instance, I am amazed at how many Americans labor under the false belief that registered voters elect our president on the first Tuesday of November each fourth year. Popular belief and acceptance aside, voters do not elect the president directly. Ask Grover Cleveland. He received one hundred thousand more votes than Benjamin Harrison in 1888 only to see Harrison inaugurated as president. Unique? Not at all. Ask Andrew Jackson. Popular elections occurred only after someone apparently decided presidents should come from states other than Virginia (eight of the first nine presidents came from that state, none since). In the first popular election (1824), John Q. Adams became president after garnering only 71 percent of the vote total of Andrew Jackson, the "loser." Ask Samuel J. Tilden. In 1876, he polled nearly three hundred thousand votes more than Rutherford B. Hayes, the "winner" who was sworn in as president.

For anthropologists, the apparent contradiction of knowing more about another culture than about our own is compounded by the frustration that often accompanies our attempts to enlighten students, citizens, and politicians. It is difficult to convince Americans that people in the New Guinea Highlands are acting rationally when they nightly seek refuge in their houses from the threat of marauding ghosts. "Guilty of primitive superstition" is the verdict, rendered by a jury addicted to horoscopes and four-leaf clovers pressed flat in books, lucky pennies in loafers, and rabbits' feet on key chains. The point is less whether the underlying beliefs are true or false, but whether or not they shape behavior. All the world's societies are peopled by rational beings in the aggregate, an essential precondition to survival. When Americans describe some other society's political or economic actions as irrational, the most telling statement is unuttered. It pertains to us. We cannot comprehend unfamiliar cultural behavior, not due to the absence of rationality among the actors, but due to our inadequate knowledge of the beliefs and institutions that generate and shape behavior. Our conclusion that the cultural behavior of others is irrational results from the tendency to explain the behavior of others with reference to our own cultural values and institutions. For anthropologists, the only thing more discouraging than our ignorance of others' values, beliefs, and institutions is our cultural tendency to ignore that ignorance.

All this brings me at last to the Imbonggu. I have lived in their presence for a significant portion of my life. Even when not sleeping with them at the base of their mountain, however, we remain joined. The Imbonggu will be with me forever, as will others of "my people" in New Guinea, Yap, and Thailand. I enjoy their company. I also benefit greatly from it in my efforts to come to grips with my own culture as it functions and evolves. That makes the Imbonggu more than friends who shared a span of years in my life. They have reshaped my worldview. They have taught me to ask questions I did not ask before I came to know them. They have taught me ways to interpret events and ideas which I would not possess without their instruction. I am convinced that all Americans would be better off if they knew the Imbonggu, or someone like them. Through the pages that follow, I hope that the reader will come to appreciate that people like the Imbonggu have much to offer in our quest to understand ourselves, our lives, and the society in which we live.

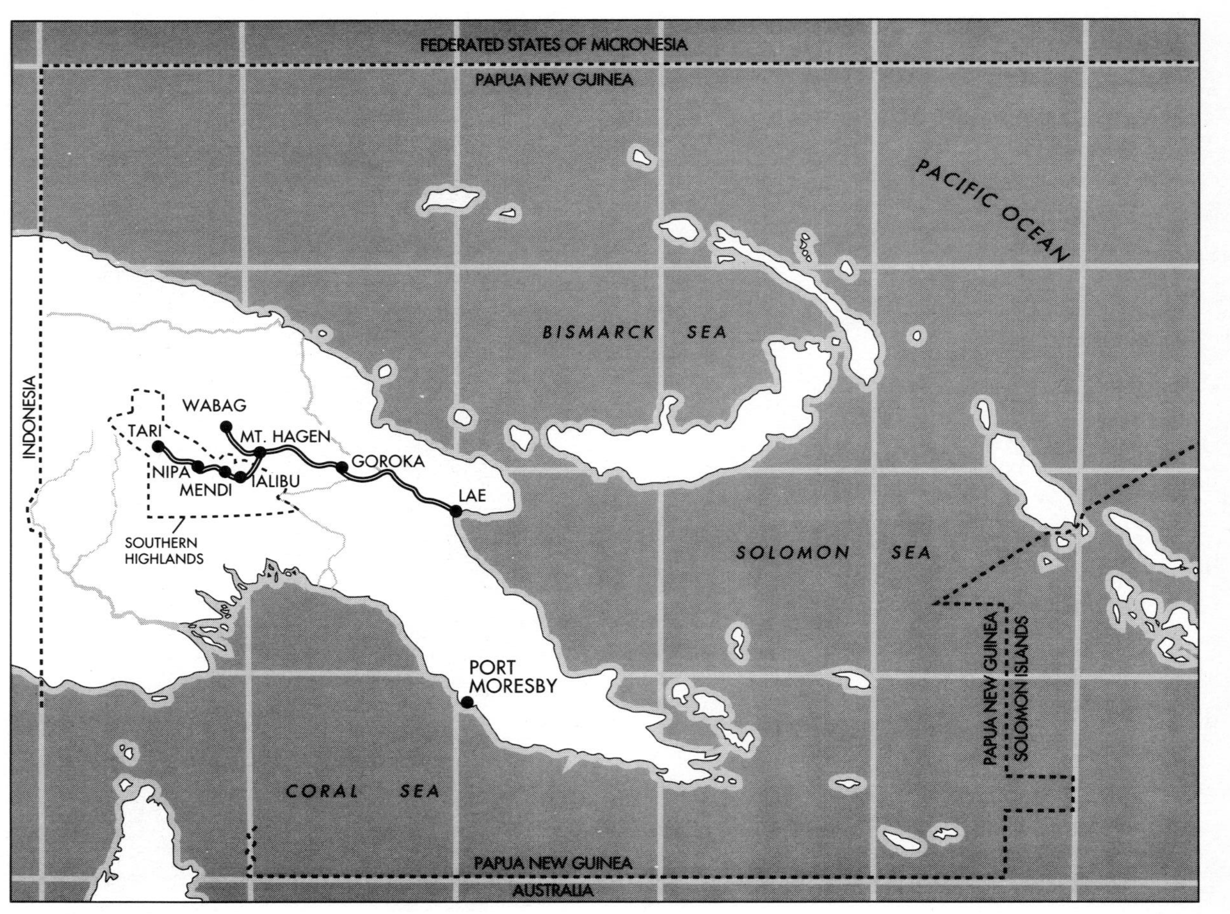
FEDERATED STATES OF MICRONESIA
PAPUA NEW GUINEA
PACIFIC OCEAN
BISMARCK SEA
INDONESIA
WABAG
TARI
MT. HAGEN
GOROKA
NIPA
MENDI
IALIBU
LAE
SOUTHERN HIGHLANDS
SOLOMON SEA
PAPUA NEW GUINEA
SOLOMON ISLANDS
PORT MORESBY
CORAL SEA
PAPUA NEW GUINEA
AUSTRALIA

New Guinea

3 / Am I There Yet?

During the two weeks I spent in Port Moresby paying the requisite courtesy calls, I made the reacquaintance of a friend from Pittsburgh. Ken Wohlberg, a doctoral student at the University of Pittsburgh, was now on the faculty at the teacher's college in Goroka. He invited me to spend a few days with him en route to the Southern Highlands.

My decision on the Southern Highlands as a field research site had finally been made. Like so many things in Papua New Guinea, it had not been easy. At the Waigani Seminar, I had met several people who had previously been only names authoring papers in professional journals. Meeting them in the flesh was exciting. It was also stressful. I repeated my "brief" ad nauseam. For Brits and Aussies, one's brief is one's raison d'être, one's professional legitimacy. Twenty different scholars would detect twenty different shortcomings in anyone's brief, most serious, many fatal. But my research proposal was sound. I had received one of only thirty-three doctoral grants awarded by the National Science Foundation to the hundreds of aspiring anthropologists who had sought the prized awards that year.

But, as I would so often conclude over the coming years, that was there, and this was here. Port Moresby provided me with my first glimpse into the petty intricacies of professional jealousies and turf wars. One expert concluded that I could not work in Mount Hagen, because Andrew and Marilyn Strathern had staked it out already. Neither Andrew nor Marilyn ever expressed such territorial concerns. Another legend in the Australian Melanesian crowd informed me that I could not expect to work in Madang because it belonged to Peter Lawrence and Louise Morauta. Neither ever expressed any concern that I would risk reprisal if I intruded on their turf. In fact, over the years all four of these people have shown themselves to be quite above the sort of petty jealousies I was erroneously led to expect from them. Based on earlier correspondence with Peter Lawrence and Andrew Strathern, I anticipated that the Southern Highlands would be the most desirable site for my research. The area was among the last to be contacted by the colonial administration. The ethnography of the region was extremely thin compared to that of the other provinces in the highlands region (Western Highlands, Eastern Highlands, Enga, and Chimbu).

Ken agreed that the choice seemed sound and invited me to make my way to the Southern Highlands via his base in Goroka, Eastern Highlands Province. He had a plan which amounted to a sadistic local rite that might be described as "testing the tenderfoot." He would take me hiking in the Okapa region. This was exciting. I had read about *kuru,* that infamous ailment of the Fore people who live there. The disease supposedly was contracted during the practice of cannibalism. I looked forward to the prospect of visiting the Fore area in the flesh, as it were.

One day at dawn, we loaded a day's food, drinking water, boots, and packs into Ken's minivan. We departed Goroka in the morning fog to make our way down the Highlands Highway, which at the time linked the port town of Lae to the frontier town of Mount Hagen in the mountainous interior of the island. The road was the best in Papua New Guinea in 1975. It boasted a gravel surface requiring constant repair efforts. In the dry season the road was the birthplace of dust storms. In the rainy season, it was often a sea of mud. When in peak condition, it was characterized by mile after mile of parallel ridges and lumps, known locally as "corrugations" or "washboarding." Prevailing wisdom held that if one's vehicle attained the proper speed, then it simply flew from the top of one ridge to the top of the next. Such ridge-hopping theoretically produced the smoothest ride. Any other speed resulted in a seemingly endless chain of minor collisions between road and vehicle, which threatened to disintegrate the vehicle while ejecting the teeth of any and all passengers. Regardless of the season, the Highlands Highway (and most other roads in Papua New Guinea) spawned a gesture I initially took to be a form of greeting, but was actually a gesture of self-defense. As two vehicles bounced toward each other from opposite directions, all passengers in the front seats pressed their flattened palms against the windscreen. This apparent gesture of greeting was in truth an essential means of reinforcing the windscreen against the hail of rocks hidden in the clouds of dust that chased vehicles up and down the highway like shadows.

To reach Okapa we had to leave the nation's only major highway. The trail that continued on to Okapa could be described as a road, but only with tongue in cheek. In truth, this road was two rock-filled parallel ruts winding through grasses frequently taller than the vehicle. The crown between the tracks was a constant threat to the undercarriage and transmission of any vehicle except the standard government-issue Toyota Land Cruiser. We followed this winding path that masqueraded as a road until Ken's minivan balked at the likely depth of the mud that consumed the road before us. We would walk the final mile to the first Fore village, a quiet collection of small houses with thatched roofs and walls of woven *pitpit* (a small cousin of bamboo). People lounged everywhere, lying on the grass or sitting around smoking. At our approach the village came to life, dashing my suspicion that I was viewing an open air rest home for *kuru* victims. We were surrounded, greeted, groped, and generally welcomed.

Ken talked with several people for a few minutes, and then announced that we were going to walk to a small stream that flowed at the bottom of a valley about a mile away horizontally and another mile away vertically from where we sat. It was agreed that several young boys would accompany us for the purpose of carrying our bags. Uncomfortable with the colonial image of a gargantuan white man being followed by small native boys, the latter carrying the cargo of the former, I declined the offer and hefted my bag. The boys smiled knowingly at one another and we set off. We had moved downhill only a few hundred meters when I grudgingly passed my bag to one of the eager boys. It was obvious that the best training for this descent would have been downhill skiing, or possibly tackling Niagara Falls in a barrel.

Both hands were required to grasp anything within reach in an effort to keep from making the entire descent in one headlong plunge. The path was slick with a thin layer of mud produced by the morning mist. The grasses refused to assist. As they slid through our grip, they left a trail of cuts and blood underlining their desire to be left undisturbed. After several minutes, it became apparent that this descent would be a constant war against locally aggressive forces of gravity. We would halt and take our bearings while we clutched ourselves to a small tree at the side of the path. Reading the path much like a golfer reads the break on a putting green, we assessed slope, distance between trees, position of trees relative to the path, and the likely speed of descent once we released our current handhold and surrendered ourselves to gravity. Calculations made, we let go of one tree and propelled ourselves in the direction of another further down the slope. The plan was to crash into the second tree or at least pass by it sufficiently closely that we could reach out and grab it, thereby interrupting and defeating gravity's evil plan for us one more time.

At the end of the descent, we found ourselves on the banks of a picturesque little stream. In an effort to relieve our canvas Vietnam-style jungle boots of their accumulated cargo of heavy mud, we waded into the water. The stream carried ice water from somewhere higher in the mountains to a tropical beach on the island's coast. I longed for hot sticky Lea Lea, smiling wallabies and all. The extent of our folly was apparent almost immediately on the climb back up the hillside. Where gravity had been a source of constant encouragement on the downward journey, it was our uncompromising enemy on the uphill return. In places, the slope was so steep that it was all but impossible to move upward. The next handhold was often out of reach. The boots, which protected the tender soles of our virgin feet, provided no purchase on the muddy trail. The young boys, who had been carrying our bags and equipment since shortly after we began our descent, now assumed the additional task of hauling us up the hill. With prehensile toes they moved from foothold to foothold and with outstretched arms offered themselves as human handholds connecting the trees that had seemed so close together on the way down. Our trip back up the hill assumed the character of a human dot-to-dot drawing.

After recovering for a few days in Goroka, Ken and I said our farewells. I headed off to the Southern Highlands, Ken's words of warning ringing in my ears. Goroka was barely three thousand feet above sea level. The villages in the regions of the Southern Highlands where I was going sat nestled at six and seven thousand feet above sea level. And the surrounding mountains soared to heights of nearly fifteen thousand feet. I was to learn that these newer mountains offered all the forms of resistance characteristic of the smaller hills of the Eastern Highlands, plus one. The greatly rarefied air of the Southern Highlands contains considerably less oxygen.

My next stop, further up the Highlands Highway, was Mount Hagen. I had made plans to meet another American there. I first met Bill Heaney at the East-West Center at the University of Hawaii. We had agreed to attempt to reestablish contact once we were both in New Guinea. A keen fisherman, Bill drove regularly from the town of Mount Hagen to several streams in the region in search of trout. I joined him twice, but not pretending to be a fisherman, I spent the afternoons lounging on the river banks drinking SP Greenies (South Pacific beer in green bottles). The higher streams of the Southern Highlands, even colder than the streams of Okapa, were ideal refrigerators.

Our second fishing trip took us to the Mendi Valley in late May 1975. At the end of the trip we made our way to the town of Mendi, the administrative headquarters of the Southern Highlands. There I met several Catholic priests from Pittsburgh with whom I talked about the Steelers and Pirates. They offered a cold SP Greenie and the latest issue of *The Sporting News,* which they received via air mail, no doubt thanks to some understanding parishioner back in western Pennsylvania. On leaving the Catholic mission, Bill and I set off in search of rooms for the night. Mendi boasted one hotel and two guesthouses. The hotel was far too expensive for our meager funds. Of the two guesthouses, one was located at the Catholic mission, but was not a true commercial enterprise open to the general populace. Besides, it had been fully occupied by visiting priests when we arrived. The other, operated by the United Church, was every bit the commerical venture. It had rooms available so we checked in. The two guesthouses represented Mendi in microcosm. The region had been colonized, in the religious sense, by the Catholics and the United Church. In order to spare local populations the stress of having to make a choice between churches, the two had charitably divided valleys and villages between themselves, and entered into something resembling a mutual nonaggression treaty. So the Catholic mission and guesthouse stood at one end of the airstrip, while the United Church enclave rested at the opposite end. We unloaded my two patrol boxes of equipment, talked for a short time, and finally went to our rooms. As I lay in my bed, I speculated on the adventure before me. I was now in the Southern Highlands. My introduction to mountains and the fine art of climbing up and down them was over. In the morning I would begin the process of paying courtesy calls to the appropriate government officers in Mendi. After that I would make my way to my final field site. Doing anthropology was the next task.

Morning arrived in Mendi with a blast of frosty air. Only a few short degrees south of the equator, solidly in the tropics, the chattering of my teeth was only slightly less violent than the shivering of the rest of my body. After a breakfast of frozen toast and eggs, Bill departed for Mount Hagen. I walked down the hill from the United Church guesthouse in the direction of the center of town. In 1975, Mendi was little more than a colonial dormitory. Few New Guineans lived in the town, except a handful of public servants and those who worked as *hausboi* or *hausmeri* to their colonial bosses (*masta* in Neo-Melanesian, the pidgin lingua franca). The town consisted of government offices, a hotel at whose bar government officers routinely became intoxicated, a golf course whose greatest hazard was the flight path which sadistically diverted small aircraft over one green at head height, two private clubs with strong whites-only preferences, and the aforementioned airstrip. Hardly a tourist mecca.

I made my way to the office of the District Commissioner. He was far too busy to speak with me at length, but approved with minimal interest my plan to make exploratory visits to both Ialibu and Tari. I would compare the two before making my final decision. I left a copy of my research proposal and letters of introduction with him and chatted briefly with his administrative assistant, a young Australian woman named Vicki Hunter. She finalized plans for me to travel to Ialibu the following morning on a government truck.

Mendi is the administrative and commercial center of the Southern Highlands Province, Papua New Guinea.

Leaving her office, I ventured into one of the three trade stores in Mendi. A trade store is a modest enterprise pretending to be a department store, but with a standard stock limited to kerosene, tinned fish, rice, tobacco, and Coca Cola. In 1975, most were operated by foreign entrepreneurs or missions. Fifteen years later, the stores look the same, but are more often in the hands of Papua New Guineans. From the shops' inventories I compiled a list of items I thought might prove useful in future. I bought some deep fried food for lunch. No more precise description is possible. About three o'clock in the afternoon I set off on the return walk to the guesthouse. I was barely at the end of town, when a white sedan appeared behind me, horn blowing. Vicki pulled up beside me, leaned from her window, and told me about a change of plans. A truck was leaving for Ialibu in just a few minutes, and I could ride on that. She would radio ahead to the ADC (Assistant District Commissioner) at Ialibu and inform him of my arrival. No, she had no idea where I would stay that night. Jack Bullock, the ADC, would sort out that small matter.

While we were talking, a blue Toyota Land Cruiser joined us. It bore the telltale adhesive symbols of the government and the spray-painted registration numbers identifying it as belonging to the ADC, Ialibu. The driver was a short muscular man with a great mop of hair seeking to escape from beneath a billed cap of the sort worn by American golfers in the 1930s. Another feature was his intense glare. This was even more notable in retrospect, for as I came to know Mali over the years, he was invariably bathed in a radiant smile that seemed perpetual. But on this day, he wore no smile. We drove to the guesthouse where he and his companion hoisted my patrol boxes onto the truck. The three of us jammed ourselves into the front seat and set off for Ialibu, a drive requiring two hours. Mali's lack of English, combined with my rudimentary Neo-Melanesian, resulted in a fairly quiet trip, save the small rocks ricocheting off our windscreen in the wake of each passing vehicle.

We arrived at Ialibu slightly after six o'clock in the evening, as twilight was setting in. We drove into the ADC's driveway, and Mali motioned for me to get out of the truck. I walked up the porch steps, knocked on the door, and found myself looking up at one of the tallest human beings I have ever encountered. I introduced myself to Jack Bullock who invited me inside where I met his wife Carolyn. He had received no radio message from Vicki, so my arrival was a bit of a surprise. But in the best Australian tradition, Jack assured me, "She'll be right, mate!" Alas, for poor Mali, my arrival in Mendi proved to be less than fortunate. We had come from Mendi in Bullock's vehicle. The same vehicle he had thought parked outside his house the entire afternoon. Poor Mali endured a tongue lashing that was impressive in both intensity and duration, although its precise content was lost on me at the moment. It was clear, however, that Mali was in very serious trouble. Trouble which he might have avoided entirely were it not for my untimely arrival in Mendi, or Vicki's chance sighting of his vehicle as he sought to flee that town undetected.

Jack and Carolyn offered me several beers and invited me to share dinner with them that evening. Jack took me in tow and we made our way to a small house which was designated as belonging to a government official who was not on staff currently. I would be able to stay there for a few days while we worked out the details of my program. We returned to Bullock's house and I was greeted by Geoff and Anne Cowper. Geoff was a patrol officer and advisor to the local government council. They joined us for beer and dinner. The Bullocks returned to Australia shortly after my arrival, but Geoff and Anne would become two of my dearest friends at Ialibu. After dinner, I returned to my temporary apartment. There was no electricity and no water. I discovered the next morning that water was available by gravity from a small tank perched on the roof of the house. It had a manual pump that demanded approximately fifty strokes to fill the tank to overflowing. I now had water with which to flush the toilet, cook, and take a shower. Cooking was accomplished atop a small kerosene stove, known as a "Bat" stove. The name came from the logo sported by the stove's small fuel tank. The stove, manufactured in Germany, was notorious for unplanned explosions and fires. I never did achieve a method of warming the freezing water to the point where I could enjoy a comfortable shower.

The next morning, I walked the few hundred meters to the main administrative office to meet Bullock. He was occupied with all the daily chores associated with his position as ADC. He inspected the police and assigned daily responsibilities ranging from issuing arrest orders to holding informal court sessions on the floor of his office or on the grass outside. The Assistant District Commissioner was God in his domain. This is in no way a judgment of Jack Bullock personally. It is merely to note the almost unlimited range of responsibility and power granted to such Australian colonial officials. Jack motioned me to join him on the veranda of the office. He asked me a few specific questions and then instructed his translator, or *tanimtok* (in Neo-Melanesian, literally "to turn the talk"), to inform the assembled crowd that I was an anthropologist. I would be at Ialibu for at least two years, and I wished to live in a village and learn the ways of the people. I tried to interject that I was only testing the water at Ialibu, that I still had to make a planned visit to Tari for the same general purpose, and that we might be moving forward a bit too quickly. In an effort to soothe the ruffled Yank before him, Jack responded in quintessential Aussie, "No worries, mate. She'll be right!"

The second morning, I awoke to a terrible pounding on my front door. Jack had arrived, along with Sirobo, his *tanimtok*. I should get dressed quickly, I was informed, as visitors were waiting. I was unprepared for what followed. The lawn outside my temporary house was packed with men. They sat cross-legged, chatting and smoking. Occasional questions in Imbonggu (the local language) were fired at Sirobo, who relayed them to Jack in Neo-Melanesian. Jack passed them on to me in Australian, which was frequently as mystifying as the Imbonggu and Neo-Melanesian. The men on the lawn were the designated representatives of their respective clans and villages. Each had come in response to yesterday's public announcement of my arrival and search for a place to live. Each had been sent to collect me and take me back to his village. This was amazing. My research brief explained that I would select a field site on the basis of several factors, including demographics, migration patterns, networks and connections to distant towns and plantations, and a host of other academic concerns. I had explained none of these factors to the men assembled before me. In fact, at this point I was incapable of doing so. Yet here I was, the object of intense competition among literally every clan and tribe in the region. Jack suggested that I go *wokabaut* and visit several villages over the next few days. Sirobo would be my guide, or he would arrange one for me. Then I could make a selection based on my own assessment. This seemed a sensible solution to me and Jack, but intense groans of displeasure emanated from the assembled multitude. Still, the decision was made and communicated to the crowd. The assembly dispersed.

About an hour later, Sirobo returned. He was accompanied by a young man named Turi who commanded a reasonable approximation of English. Turi would take me to visit two villages initially, Nagop and Tona. We walked northeast from the government station. The distance to Nagop was only about four kilometers, but it took much longer than I had anticipated. Every twenty meters or so we encountered another group of strolling Imbonggu who greeted us with smiles, pressed Turi to explain who I was, and demanded to know how it had come about that I was with him. I began to have opportunities to employ my budding Neo-Melanesian and even learned a few words of Imbonggu.

The walk to Nagop took nearly two and one-half hours. As the months wore on, and I became less of a novelty (and finally none at all), the same walk required barely an hour. We left the road behind and turned onto a small path strewn with rocks and slick with a thin film of mud. The center of the path was marked by a miniature canyon carved by the runoff of the nearly constant drizzle. I would come to learn that the path was more frequently a stream bed. We walked through more mud, up a few small hills, and crossed a few more streams. We walked through *kunai* grass that was frequently as tall as I. We encountered dogs at every turn. Scrawny, mangy dogs, with great patches of smooth skin where fur should have been. They occasionally barked, but more often skulked away with a whine when Turi hurled stones in their general direction. Occasionally we met a young woman walking in the company of a pig, the two linked by a woven cord connecting feminine wrist to porky ankle. As we continued walking we heard dozens of pigs grunting and snorting out of sight in the grass. A half-mile from the road, we crossed one last stream. As we went up the final hill into the village I encountered my first Imbonggu house. It was low to the ground, square at one end and rounded at the other. The sides were about five meters in length. The squared-off front end rose to a central peak about six feet in height. The peak marked one end of a spine that extended to the rounded end of the house, becoming ever lower as it went, so the rear of the house was no more than four feet high. The roof was thatched with grass hanging over and beyond the walls, falling to within a foot of the ground. Flat rocks were placed irregularly over the roof in no apparent pattern. What I initially took to be weights aimed at holding the thatch in place against the winds were in fact normal roof repairs to prevent leaks. The rocks compressed the thatch keeping it damp in critical places where leaks developed after days of no rain.

We sat before the house on the grass, still damp from the morning dew and fog. We were joined by several men as they ambled by. Each asked the same question, "Who is the white man, and what is he doing here?" The question was never put forth in tones of anger or threat. Rather, it was accompanied by an unmistakable sense of skepticism and doubt. The appearance of a white man in an Imbonggu village nearly always implied trouble or at the very least some inconvenience or unpleasantness. However, most such special occasions were announced and scheduled well in advance. Tax collections, village census, or political lectures though seldom anticipated with joy were equally seldom surprises. But a strange white man dressed in the same field clothes as an Australian patrol officer and entering the village unannounced could only mean one thing. Someone was going to be arrested. All men accepted that arrest was an ever-present, if highly unlikely, possibility. Every Imbonggu man I would meet was guilty of violating one law or another. Many failed to pay their annual taxes, either out of poverty or mere refusal to give away their scarce and hard-earned money. The annual tax hit the older and more prominent men hardest. The tax was determined by the number of wives a man had. The annual head tax per adult male was seven *kina* (about seven American dollars). He was obligated to pay an additional fifty *toea* (about fifty cents) for each wife. For old Nagop, with fifteen wives, his tax bill was fourteen kina fifty toea. His income was zero. Other men routinely refused to appear at the local school, several kilometers away, to cut grass and repair fences each Monday.

There was a multitude of other minor offenses that could result in arrest. The only thing nearly as universal as the refusal of Imbonggu men to obey these irritating local ordinances was the reluctance of the police to enforce them. Australian patrol officers and government officials made lists of names and issued arrest warrants in quantities that sometimes seemed to duplicate the census. Daily, the police sadly reported their inability to track down the cunning fugitives. I once observed a comical situation in which a policeman reported to an Australian patrol officer that he had searched for days for a man to be arrested on charges of having stolen a pig. But the fugitive, a man named Yama, was exceptionally cunning and seemed always one step ahead of the increasingly frustrated policeman. The patrol officer heard the familiar report and nodded in resigned understanding. He told the policeman to forget Yama for the moment and to concentrate on another matter in a different village. The policeman saluted smartly, turned on his heel, and left the office. In doing so he brushed past a gentleman standing just inside the door. His name was Yama, the very same man who had evaded the police for days. Yama's reason for being in the office that morning was to demand the arrest of a man who he was convinced had stolen his pig!

Once Turi had dispelled the initial fear of arrest, several men joined us on the grass. Each carefully removed the machete (known locally as a bush knife) from the wide bark belt that served to hold in place the normal wardrobe of Imbonggu men, a long woven piece of cloth in front and a bunch of wide green cordyline leaves that covered the backside. When sitting down, the skirt was held tightly against the genitals with one hand to ensure modesty. The men then sat cross-legged and observed, asking occasional questions about what I planned to do over the next two years. Where was I from? Pittsburgh, America. Knowing nods, without the slightest hint that no one present had even the faintest clue where Pittsburgh was. Most of the men present were deathly afraid to go to Mount Hagen, only forty kilometers away. Was I married? Yes. That my wife was in Australia seemed to cause little interest. How many wives did I have? Only one. Why? Do you really want to live in a village house? My yes generated laughter and shaking heads. Disbelief was evident. Did I really want to eat village foods? More doubt. And so it went for several hours. The same questions were asked again and again as new visitors joined our circle and others departed. At about one o'clock the afternoon clouds began to form. Turi suggested that we return to the station at Ialibu before the afternoon rains began to fall.

As we walked back to the road, a young man named Naba accompanied us. He suggested that Turi and I return to Nagop in three days. We could watch him kill a pig and cook it. The pig had raided a neighbor's garden. The angry neighbor had hurled a rock at the pig to frighten it. With unpredictable accuracy, the rock had struck the pig in its right foreleg. The leg was broken. The pig would have to be destroyed. Naba had exploded in anger and demanded compensation. The neighbor agreed to the demand. He would pay for the pig. In return, he would receive some of the meat when the pig was cooked. Naba stressed that I should bring my camera and take pictures of the activities. In addition, Tie would be there, as would Mare. Tie and Mare were about nineteen years old, and the two most beautiful unmarried girls in the village, according to Naba. They also happened to be his sisters. Sisters in Imbonggu may be somewhat more distantly related than sisters in American society. Tie was the daughter of Naba's father, who had two wives. Naba was born of one, Tie of the other. When Naba's father died, Tie's mother (his second wife) was remarried, to the younger brother of Naba's father as his second wife. Her new husband (Naba's uncle in American terms, but his father in Imbonggu) already had one wife by whom he had produced a daughter (Mare). This was intensely exciting. Real anthropological kinship. One man with two fathers, one of whom was an uncle, and two sisters, one of whom was actually a half-sister and the other a cousin/step-sister. At that moment I actually began to feel like an anthropologist! No taller. No straighter. Just more anthropological. I accepted Naba's invitation eagerly, unable to wait to jump in and get my feet wet. My first morning in the field, and I had already managed to meet dozens of men, arranged to witness my first pig slaughter, and begun to fill out my first Imbonggu genealogy. As we walked toward the road, Turi helped me with a rough sketch map of the village. I asked Turi which house was his. "I don't live in Nagop. I live in Tona. We will go there another day." As we left the village, walking past the same houses we had encountered earlier as we entered Nagop, Turi noted the names of the owners and occupants for me. "That one belongs to Mali. You know him, he is Bullock's driver," Turi remarked casually. What an incredible coincidence, I thought to myself. "That house belongs to Sirobo. He has another house nearby for his two wives, his children and his pigs." As I wrote the name in my notes, I said to Turi, "What a coincidence. Isn't that the same name as the *tanimtok* at the government station?" "Oh, yes," Turi replied, "it is the same man." Coincidence, indeed.

The next day Turi took me to Tona village, about a kilometer further from the station than Nagop. Tona is home to the Imbi, one of many localized social groups collectively defined as the Imbonggu. The first house we encountered upon entering Tona belonged to Turi's father, Yombi. He greeted me warmly, and sat down with us on the grass before his house. He sheepishly confessed that he would have offered me a cigarette, but for the fact he had none to offer at the moment. I told him that I did not smoke. He nodded his head in approval. Having been alerted to the fact that everyone smokes in the highlands of New Guinea, I had purchased several cartons of cigarettes and chewing tobacco (*muruk* in Neo-Melanesian as well as a brand name). As if the contradiction did not exist, Yombi eagerly accepted one of my cigarettes. He sent his young daughter Indipendo scurrying into the house from which she soon returned with a glowing ember from the hearth. Yombi puffed the cigarette to life, leaned back, and exhaled.

As in Nagop, we were joined by passersby who listened for a time, asked the now-familiar questions, and then went about their business. Wareia invited me to go hunting with him. Kagu offered to show me some kina shells. Another promised to show me his magic stones. Wakea would instruct me in his love magic. All the men present eagerly agreed that Wakea possessed the most potent love magic in the village. How else could a wrinkled man of eighty years be married to a beautiful young woman in her twenties? Under the circumstances, it was only natural that Arume should insist that I meet Peni, his beautiful and unmarried daughter.

Even the gods seemed favorably disposed to Tona, for on this afternoon there was no rain. We wandered about the village. We shared sugar cane. Invitations to participate in village activities seemed endless and sincere. As we walked past one small grove of trees near his house, Yombi suggested that it was a perfect site for a house. He had been intending to build his own new house there, but had not yet found the time. Why didn't I build my own house on that spot? I assured Yombi that I would think about it, but I could not make the decision for a few more days. As we walked back to the station, I asked Turi where we might go tomorrow. What about the village between Nagop and the station, the one known as Ama? "Oh, no. You could not live there. It is full of sorcerers and very bad people." What about Piambil village? "No. It is full of thieves, cannibals, and very bad people." I resolved to check with Jack Bullock about other possibilities in the Ialibu Basin.

That night, over the usual number of SP greenies, I talked with Jack Bullock and Geoff Cowper about the villages I had seen as well as some of the ones I was interested in seeing. Nagop and Tona were a bit far from the station, and not much was known about either. Piambil, on the other hand, was very well known to both Jack and Geoff. Close to the station, it provided the bulk of the government labor force. As a result, it was atypical. Many of its official residents were in fact nonresidents living on the government station at Ialibu (pronounced ya´-li-boo). Also, by virtue of all the wage income, the life-style of those living in Piambil was not as traditional as that in most other villages in the basin. Ama was even closer to the station, but provided almost no laborers. Actually, Ama was not Ama at all. That name belonged to one of the several clans that inhabited the village. The village itself was known to its residents as Imi. As I would discover over and over again, this was not the only instance of government officers' mistaken designation of people and places in Ialibu. A third village, Kapogapobil, was the base of a Christian evangelistic mission. As a result, it was the least traditional village in the region. Each evening, the government station at Ialibu was treated to a seemingly endless concert of Christian hymns. The women of the village all wore tops as dictated by the missionary. All this Christian zeal was too much. Kapogapobil and anthropology seemed an unlikely match. Months later I had the opportunity to watch a public ceremony in which some women from Kapogapobil danced. They were immediately recognizable. In the sea of bare-breasted female dancers, only they wore bras. As I stood taking photographs of the women, the missionary approached and informed me with conviction, "Breasts are objects of lust." Uncertain whether he was explaining the bizarre appearance of the women of Kapogapobil or commenting on my photographic interest in the uncovered breasts of the women from the other villages, I responded that breasts might be objects of lust in America but probably not in Ialibu. My suggestion was not well received. Nor was my unfortunately indelicate suggestion that lust, like beauty, probably resides in the eye of the beholder. We never spoke again.

Jack and Geoff suggested that I try Kuminge village. Like Tona and Nagop, it had no resident missionary (nor even a village church), no school, no aid post, and no government laborers other than Mali and Sirobo. The next day, Turi agreed to take me to Kuminge if I insisted. I was impressed with his willingness to show me another village, fully aware of the possible risk that I might settle there rather than in Tona, or even Nagop. Although eventually I did not choose to build my house in Kuminge, I found myself returning there several times over the years, often in the company of Turi's new wife whom he married in late 1975. They gave birth to their first child in August 1976, and his wife Nabene and I occasionally walked together as she took her new son to visit his grandmother in her home village, Kuminge. Just one more strange coincidence, no doubt.

After visiting several villages, I came to a major decision. I had come to think a great deal of Ialibu. The Imbonggu enticed me with their smiles. And the colonial Australian contingent of government officers enticed me with their SP greenies. I decided not even to go to Tari for a comparative visit. Ialibu had already won me over. It helped that I was the first anthropologist to work in the Ialibu Basin, whereas Tari had hosted several anthropologists before me. Without even recognizing the transformation, I had become as territorial as those first anthropologists I had met in Port Moresby two months earlier. Ialibu was now my field site, and the Imbonggu had become "my people."

Christian modesty and Imbonggu dress

Anthropologists tend to assume a protective and proprietary interest in their people. Others often perceive our sincere commitment differently. Vine Deloria once wrote, "Into each life, it is said, some rain must fall. . . . But Indians have been cursed above all people in history. Indians have anthropologists" (1969:83). This protective tendency of anthropologists also presents risks to anthropologists themselves, a fact brought home to me years later by a friend and colleague, Luis Quiros. A political scientist, Quiros held the view that anthropologists were essentially useless in the policy-making process because they suffered from "my people syndrome." He meant that anthropologists too often respond to policy suggestions with the time honored, "That won't work, because my people think this, or my people do that." He was convinced that until anthropologists developed the extended view of the political process common to political scientists we would forever operate on the fringe of the policy process and be perceived as nothing more than a hindrance to that process. Even worse, as long as we are perceived to be little more than obstructionist, we are unlikely to join the inner circles in which policy is created. Thus we will be unable to contribute to the policies affecting our people. In that sense, we fail them. We are reduced to offering tardy and ineffective protests from the sidelines after the event.

Luis Quiros, political scientist, would not teach me what anthropology should be for another six years, however. In the meantime I had found my place and my people. The Imbonggu had been tucked timelessly away in the Ialibu Basin of what had once been the Australian Territory of Papua, but was now the independent nation of Papua New Guinea. They had been waiting for me for centuries, and at last I had found them.

4 / What Do You Do When You Meet a White Man?

We have no way of knowing precisely how long human beings have lived in the highlands of New Guinea. No one doubts it has been a long time, however. Archaeologist Jack Golson has excavated prehistoric agricultural systems at Kuk, about eighty miles northeast of the Ialibu Basin. Kuk's drainage ditches are evidence of an agricultural system that is probably among the most ancient in the world, possibly as old as nine thousand years (Golson 1982:119). Other sites have yielded less direct evidence in the sense that they contain no human remains or artifacts. Cave sites littered with the remains of animals known to have been domesticated thousands of years ago provide a hint that people may have entered the highlands as much as thirty thousand years ago, probably earlier. Most of the thirty thousand years would have offered little in the way of change, and what did occur would have been so slow as to be unnoticeable from the perspective of an individual Papuan. Diseases no doubt raged from time to time. Warfare likely would have been a common phenomenon. Only the shift to agriculture would have radically altered the shape and pace of life.

There was, of course, one notable exception. In a world of more or less homogeneous Papuans and Melanesians, people no doubt felt a sense of certainty and predictability. Security in numbers, in a sense. But by the early 1930s this familiar world was on the brink of an upheaval no Imbonggu, or any other highlander, could have predicted in the wildest dream (Schieffelin and Crittenden 1991). A single event, repeatedly reenacted across the highlands, remains etched in the memories of thousands of men and women, including the Imbonggu. Yombi was probably about forty-five years of age when I first met him in 1975. It was likely he had seen his first white man about forty years earlier. No Imbi born prior to 1970 is aware of his or her age or date of birth, except in the relative sense of being older than someone or younger than someone else. There is a touch of humor in even these relative dating techniques. Yombi never said, "I was as old as so and so" when some event occurred. Rather, he said, "I was the size of Ope when I saw my first white man." Age and size are linked by the Imbi in the apparent misapprehension that age and size correlate directly. The Imbi know better, of course. But as systems go, this one meets most needs. I knew Ope to be five years old, thus it seems likely that Yombi encountered his first white man sometime during the early 1930s.

Australian exploration patrols in New Guinea were probably the last great treks of discovery in the modern world. Even after World War II, Australian colonial officers continued to encounter previously unknown tribes living in the unexplored mountains of New Guinea. Reports of first contact continued to appear as late as the mid-1980s. The early patrols of New Guinea are legendary. The accounts of explorers such as Ivan Champion (1932), Jack Hides (1935), James Sinclair (1966), and the Leahy brothers are packed with excitement (Connolly and Anderson 1987; Leahy 1991). The Staniford-Smith Patrol travelled considerably to the southwest of Imbonggu territory in 1911. The Fox brothers travelled well to the north of Mount Giluwe in 1934. Hides and O'Malley explored the Erave region, southwest of the Imbonggu in 1934. In 1933 and 1934, the Leahy brothers walked southwestward from Mount Hagen (Leahy 1991:171–201). It is known that they penetrated as far as Mount Giluwe. They climbed the mountain and determined its elevation to be 13,770 feet, although they rejected their own finding in favor of an earlier estimate in excess of 14,000 feet above sea level. They also walked around the flanks of Mount Ialibu.

Yombi had heard stories of white men before he saw them for the first time. It is quite possible that the stories of those wild and frightening creatures were passed from the southwest and referred to the earlier Staniford-Smith and Hides-O'Malley patrols. Or the stories might have been generated by the Fox patrol that went north of Ialibu. But Yombi's initial personal encounter with white men was almost certainly the Leahy brothers explorations of 1933 and 1934. The brothers definitely entered the Ialibu Basin and came closer to the Imbi than any of the earlier patrols. And they scared the hell out of Yombi. "I was the size of Ope when the first white men came to Ialibu. I was very frightened. I hid in the *pitpit*. I saw the white men, but they could not see me. They only walked through, and did not stop." Yombi ran to his house in fear. Other people were also beginning to recover from the sight of these foreign spirits. What did they want? More important, what would they do? Was it a sign? Would someone die? These spirits had walked southward from Mount Giluwe, and it was a well-known fact that to see the spirits living on Mount Giluwe resulted in death. Were these strange white men some bizarre manifestation of those dreadful mountain spirits? People were terror-stricken. Fortunately, the creatures passed through quickly and did not return.

Yombi's life resumed its normal pace for several years. "When I was Purul's size [Purul was Yombi's fifteen-year-old son] some other young boys and I were building a dam across a small stream. We heard a very loud noise we had never heard before. We covered one ear and put the other to the ground, but heard nothing. Then we listened to the water, but heard nothing. We feared that spirits were angry that we had disturbed the ground and the stream to make a dam so we could swim in the water. We heard the noise again. This time we looked in the sky. It was the first airplane I had seen. We were all very frightened, and ran into the bush. I ran to some young men, but they chased me away. They were afraid the flying spirit would follow me to where they were hiding and kill them." The flying spirit disappeared, leaving incomprehension in its wake. Once again people were beset by fears. What was this new visitor? What would come of its visit? Would it return? And what would it do next time? "Shortly after this, another airplane appeared. But this time it dropped something from the sky. We did not know of bombs at that time. But the bomb made a great noise and cloud of smoke. Ten men and ten women were killed. That bomb landed at Muli. Later we learned that another bomb had fallen at Pangia." World War II had come to the Imbonggu before they had come to know of that larger world seemingly so intent on destroying itself.

"A few years later, the white men came back. They had walked all the way from Mount Hagen. They set up a camp at Piambil. We all went to look at them. Some *kanaka* who were with the white men told me to wash their clothes and dishes. I was afraid to refuse. So I worked in the white men's camp. But while I was there, a fight broke out between the white men and some men from Kuminge. One man from Kuminge was killed. The white men ran away, back to Mount Hagen, but not before I had run back to Nagop. I thought, maybe the white men will kill all of us. But they did not come back for a long time. Several years later, another group of white men came to Ialibu. I don't know if they were government or mission. But they burned all the men's houses and spirit houses." In addition, sacred stones were broken or thrown into streams. The missionaries were paving the way for Christianity. The moment the destruction and sacrilege began, word spread like lightning through the villages. Men hid many of their most cherished items, especially their magical stones and the skulls of their ancestors. After I had lived with the Imbi for nearly a year, they had come to trust me enough to show me the sacred items they had hidden away and that had escaped the combined wrath of God and colonialism.

After all these brief and seemingly random events, the white men finally came with the obvious intention of remaining. They constructed official buildings, houses, and missions five miles from Nagop and Tona. Eventually, they set about building an airstrip. By this time, Yombi was an adult of considerable importance. The white men approached him, through a *tanimtok,* and told him that he should bring some of his men and help build the airstrip. Afraid to refuse, several Imbi men assisted in the construction. When the runway was completed, Yombi was given a frightening reward. With other influential local men who had supplied laborers for the airstrip, he was herded into an airplane one day. He was terrified. Did the white men intend to carry him away and eat him? Would they throw him from the plane like some human bomb? The door was slammed shut. Too afraid to speak, the men sat in mute amazement as the engines chugged to life. The plane shook so violently that Yombi feared it would break apart. Then as he and his comrades looked out the window, the plane began to race along the ground. Unable to look forward, all they could witness was their world racing before their eyes as it flew past the windows on the side of the plane. He was certain they would all die. But then the plane lifted into the air. Yombi's muscles tensed. His ears ached. The plane banked to one side, and he fought to move away from the window, so certain was he that he would fall out. But then he saw things he recognized as houses. He also saw people beneath him running to hide from the *balus* spirit, as he had done so many years before.

It is sheer delight to listen to Yombi tell his story to a house crowded with young children. Eyes are fixed on him in disbelief and admiration. When I first heard Yombi's story, no other Imbi had ever set foot in an airplane. And like those Americans who refused for years to believe that astronauts had walked on the moon, there remain Imbi who are quite convinced that Yombi is the victim of some tragic delusion. But by late 1975, Yombi had experienced it all. As a terrified boy he had hidden from the first white men he had ever seen. He had witnessed a bird or spirit never seen before. He had seen bombs fall from the sky and kill innocent men and women, who were probably hiding in the grass, frozen in terror. He had seen a white man kill an Imbonggu with a rifle. And finally, trapped in the gut of the *balus* beast, he had soared above the villages of Ialibu and peered down at people racing to hide in the grass. When Yombi describes those early encounters with white men, he admits sheepishly that he did not know about white men and airplanes at the time. But he retells the events vividly, and with a touch of disbelief at his ignorance of the shape life had taken a mere forty miles away.

Eleven years after Yombi first told me his story, I was back in America teaching anthropology to students at the University of Wyoming. Each semester I screened a film called *First Contact*. It was released in 1983 in Australia. In one of those wonderful events more attributable to good luck than planning, the original motion picture film shot by the Leahy brothers during their earlier treks through the highlands (near Imbonggu but not in it) was discovered uncatalogued in the Australian national film archive. Two film specialists were given the enviable task of creating something from this unexploited gold mine. They returned to the regions and people immortalized on the Leahy brothers' film. They sought out as many surviving highlanders as they could who were witness to the events filmed by Mick Leahy. The final product meshes the original black and white footage with modern color footage which was shot during interviews with people presenting their recollections of events of those early treks through the highlands. My anthropology students sat spellbound as the story unfolded, as disbelieving of the Papuan response to white intruders as the Papuans had been disbelieving of the intruders themselves. But the Papuan accounts are so compelling that the viewer inevitably becomes caught up in the entire surreal experience. As the film unfolds, comprehension of the true nature of these new white men also begins to emerge. In an effort to determine if the newcomers were men or spirits, a group of men followed one of the Leahy brothers into the bush one day. He went to defecate, no doubt hoping for some measure of privacy. But as all highlands anthropologists know, there is no privacy to be had there. His work finished, the unsuspecting Leahy strode back to the camp. The three men who had observed him from the bush moved to investigate the product of his labor. They raced back to their houses, assembled a mass of people, and made a startling announcement: "Their skin is different . . . but their shit smells just like ours" (Connolly and Anderson 1983).

Like his highlands brothers portrayed in *First Contact,* Yombi had come to know a great deal about white men. But there was still much he did not know. And much of what he knew to be true of white men made no sense to him. And now, the latest in the unexpected and incomprehensible: Yombi had an anthropologist living next door. And who could predict what this latest white man would do?

5 / A Home Away from Home

It was agreed that Yombi would build my house on his favored spot in view of both mountains, Giluwe and Ialibu. He would organize all the phases of the project. Men would provide wood for the frame and women would provide grass for the thatch. Young boys would cut *pitpit* for walls which would be plaited by young men, and several young girls would plant flowers around the house. Nabene would make a small garden of sweet potato, and Yombi would plant sugar cane among the sweet potato mounds in order that I be able to extend appropriate hospitality to visitors.

The site was cleared, and the floor plan was laid out on the peeled-back earth. We would need approximately thirty straight poles for the walls. Another thirty for the floor, and a dozen longer poles for the roof. The poles would come from the sides of Mount Ialibu which towered over the village. About twelve men would each make three separate trips to the mountain to procure the necessary timber. Each of the men who provided materials would receive two kina in payment. All the construction would be done by Yombi, with Turi's help. Yombi would receive thirty kina on completion of the structure. In addition, I would pay his annual head tax assessed by the government at the rate of seven kina per adult man and fifty toea per wife. Since Yombi had only one wife, his tax was seven kina fifty toea each year. After all the negotiations were complete, we made our first foray to the mountain on July 28. Anda, by virtue of his experience and seniority, was the expedition's leader. We were accompanied by eleven other men (including Turi), three small boys who were intending to hunt birds with their small bows and arrows, and far too many yapping dogs to have made bird hunting a realistic pursuit. At about a mile from the village, the path began gradually to slope upward. Grasslands gave way to small vegetable gardens more comfortable with the slightly higher and drier soil.

Mount Ialibu is a classic volcano in geological terms. When viewed from directly above, the mountain presents the image of a central point with long thin arms radiating outward from it. The runoff of constant heavy rain has produced several deep gorges separated by ridges. The slope from ridge top to gorge bottom often approaches the vertical and is always frighteningly steep. The mountain's peak is the center of a system in social as well as geological terms. As the physical center of a social universe, Ialibu's summit may also be visualized as the center of a huge pie. The pie is cut into slices by the rugged ridges stretching outward from the peak, each slice coinciding with the territorial domain of a different social group. The boundary between one slice/territory and another is usually a ridge top. Thus each clan's territory narrows as one moves from the floor of the Ialibu Basin to the peak of Mount Ialibu. Moving deeper into a clan's territory, one eventually be-

Anda led us up the forested slopes of Mount Ialibu to cut poles for my house.

comes entrapped in a rocky streambed that climbs the steep mountain by way of a narrowing corridor bounded by two nearly vertical forested walls. The climb up such a wall terminates in a ridge top seldom wider than the footpath along the spine of the ridge, which then plunges to the depth of another stream's canyon belonging to a neighboring clan.

When setting out from a village to climb the mountain, people either make their way up the streambed or along the top of a ridge. Either way, the trek is arduous. Women normally travel the streambeds because their primary reason for going to the mountain is to harvest garden vegetables. Gardens tend to be located near the bottoms of the miniature canyons. Men, on the other hand, tend to go to the mountains either to collect firewood or timber for building. The gardens cease to thrive after a climb of only a few hundred meters above the level of the village, while the forest continues to the very summit of the mountain. The nature of the forest cover changes with increasing elevation, however. The choice of whether to follow a stream or follow a ridge is thus determined less by ease of movement and more by the type of wood required.

Following the spine of a ridge toward the summit of Mount Ialibu is a nerve-racking experience, at least for those who have not been doing it since the age of ten. The path is slippery with moisture and mud most of its length. The constant shroud of fog and mist provides the perfect conditions for the heavy growth of mosses at certain elevations. Walking through a moss forest is a bizarre experience. The path becomes a moist sponge that gurgles water under every footfall. The trunks and branches of trees are covered with moss. The trees stand out as silent skeletons in the chilly fog floating eerily among them. The dank air permeates everything, including intruding humans. Sounds are muffled, as if the spirits of the place demand silence in their presence. The birds, which sing so lustily above and below the moss zones, do not venture inside. Like the birds themselves, even their calls do not enter the moss forest. Silence is total.

Men walking in the mossy regions of the mountain are also conspicuously quiet. No one talks. In part it is out of fear of the malicious spirits residing there. They are known to cause intruders to trip and fall over the branches and vines concealed by the layers of moss on the forest floor. Physical injury is not the only risk. Men often become disoriented in the deathly silence of this misty, damp forest. Stories abound of men lost in the moss zones who become disoriented and frightened, are eventually accosted by spirits, and are finally driven mad with fright. Wisdom demands that men pass through the moss forest with dispatch, making as little noise as possible in an effort to avoid attracting the attention of spirits.

Walking the streambeds one occasionally happens on shallow pools behind small dams of rocks and mud. In the mountain's desire for symmetry, each such dam along a streambed is accompanied by a scar in the ridge top above. As bits of the ridge give way and plunge to the stream below, they leave a broken trail behind them. Walking along the ridge, one frequently encounters a vertical wall marking the site of such geological mishaps. To overcome these obstacles only two strategies exist. One is to mark a new path to the side of the obstacle. But given the narrow width of the ridge top and the steepness of the slope from ridge to streambed, this is very often impossible. The second solution is the construction of a ladder that allows one to climb over the vertical wall of earth.

After an hour of climbing, we encountered the first of these ladders. I began to have second thoughts about the wisdom of building a house in Tona if climbing this ladder was a necessary first step. The base of the ladder was the width of the path. If it slipped either way, a streambed beckoned three or four hundred feet below. The young boys were ordered to climb up the ladder first while two men held it in place. Once up the ladder the boys held it in place from the top as the older men climbed up. When only two or three men remained below, Turi indicated that I should climb the ladder. I gripped the first rung, which was cold and slippery. The rungs were fastened to the two vertical poles by means of vines. They were unevenly spaced, and the first one gave way slightly when I placed my weight firmly on it. I weighed nearly eighty pounds more than most of the men in our group. Would this flimsy ladder support my weight? If not, what were the chances that my companions would be able to keep me from plunging to one of the streams below? Situations such as this illustrate the power of peer pressure. Urged on by a dozen Imbonggu men and three Imbonggu boys, I climbed the ladder.

Some undetermined distance along the ridge path, we finally reached our destination. The trees at the site were tall, straight, and thin, exactly the size and shape required for the poles to support my house. The young boys and the dogs disappeared into the forest to hunt for birds whose plumes someday would be worn atop a headdress, if luck was with the hunters. The men feverishly set to work. Abruptly, the gentle noises of the forest, birds singing and leaves rustling in the breeze, gave way to the assault of man on nature. The sharp crack of axes invading trees was followed by the even louder sound of broken and dying trees crashing to the ground, unsuccessfully attempting to maintain their balance by grabbing hold of their standing neighbors as they fell. Like the hairless patches on the mangy dogs, there was now a small treeless patch in the forest. We cut thirty-three trees in less than an hour. Each man bundled three trees together and bound them with the same forest vines which had connected the trees in life. Each man hoisted the bundle of house poles on one shoulder and his axe over the other, the head of the axe beneath the bundle of trees for support. By exerting pressure downward on both the bundle of poles and the axe handle, each carrier balanced his load. We returned by a different route that took us closer to Nagop. Even the most daring of the men chose to avoid the risks of climbing down ladders and sliding off ridge tops.

For the next several days, Yombi worked diligently on the actual construction of my house. It was erected to my floor plan, rather than the traditional Imbonggu design. I needed a taller ceiling to accommodate my greater height and extended floor space to accommodate my bookshelves and a small desk at which to write my research notes daily. The house was twelve by fifteen feet, or close to it, and divided internally into two rooms of nearly equal dimensions and joined by a narrow door. One room contained my bed, desk, storage boxes, and so forth. The other was empty except for a central hearth dug into the floor. Entry to the house was via this uncluttered room.

Poles were placed about every eighteen inches around the perimeter of the floor plan, with one wider gap in spacing to accommodate the door. Woven and plaited bamboo wall panels were placed on both the outside and inside of this rectangle of poles. Moss was stuffed between them for insulation. Women collected bundles of *kunai* grass from outside the village. The grass was tied into large bundles and carried to the village by the young daughters of the grass cutters. One of the many moments of joy given me by the Imbonggu was the arrival of the grass for my roof. As I sat before Pera's house one afternoon, we looked across the village at a long line of giggling cones of grass, atop small brown feet, marching in single file toward my house. Each girl had tied her bundle of grass near the top with vines. She then fanned the bundle outward at the untied end and rested the tied end atop her head. The unbound ends of the grass surrounded the little bodies like a cape. The girls peered through small slits in the bundles of grass as they walked onto the ceremonial ground at the center of the village. They giggled as small children ran to hide behind their mothers' legs at the sight of walking bundles of grass. Dogs barked their confusion, lending even greater hilarity to the scene. The bundles were eventually piled before my roofless house, and a dozen giggling girls raced into hiding.

A week later, the grass was in place atop the roof, and the house was complete. Two other buildings to the rear of the house completed the larger estate. One was a shower stall, containing an apparatus with a bucket (complete with shower head at the bottom), which was hoisted above my head by a rope. The water, heated over my kerosene stove, provided a comfortable (if short) shower. The bucket contained enough water to wet myself down initially. After halting the flow of water, I lathered up with soap and scrubbed thoroughly. The water was turned on again to rinse off the soap. The second small structure enclosed my toilet. This structure was the talk of the village. A pit three feet square was dug to a depth of about six feet.

Young girl delivering thatch for the roof of my house

My house in Tona

Across it were placed several poles in two perpendicular layers, so as to leave a central square about one foot on each side. Directly above it was placed a large square box. This thronelike toilet seat, the only one of its kind in the village, was destined to be a favored stop on the village tour when visitors came to see exactly how the village white man lived. The entire apparatus was surrounded by four walls and a flat, angled roof. Crowds of children hung around laughing and giggling as the novel structure took shape. Imbonggu toilet houses were not nearly so elaborate, or so interesting. They normally consisted of no more than the covered pit with no box to sit on. The user merely squatted over the hole. Imbonggu toilet shelters were never fully enclosed, nor did they sport a roof like mine. The Imbonggu built their toilet houses as a concession to the demands of the colonial health authorities in the latter's urge to achieve sanitation. The toilets were indeed sanitary, primarily because the Imbonggu seldom used them. Fear of sorcery was so great that men believed it was safer to slip off into the grass to relieve themselves than to provide sorcerers with the necessary fecal material by depositing it neatly in a toilet.

When my estate was completed, I enjoyed a view of Mount Ialibu from my front door and a spectacular view of Mount Giluwe from the rear of my house. The two mountains, towering over me and the Imbonggu, provided the illusion of protection and a sense of security. They also defined the limits of the universe by presenting visually impassable barriers. While the two mountains had always provided the Imbonggu with the same physical barriers against outside intrusion, they had not always guaranteed the total security I sensed. Occasionally in the past, as Tobil described it, these two quiet mountains themselves had been the most dangerous and threatening neighbors.

6 / Mountains at War

The Imbi live at the top of the world, or at least the world as they know it. Only spirits and the mountains themselves live closer to the heavens. To the Imbi, home is a rain-soaked basin nearly seven thousand feet above the sea, which most have never seen and few ever will. The Ialibu Basin is wet, cold, and constantly shrouded in rain and mist.

Viewed from the air, home to the Imbi is a flat table, covered with a lush green carpet sporting occasional patches of deeper green. Other patches reflect the color of the sky, and all are connected by meandering brown lines. The carpet that appears so gentle from above is rather hostile on the ground. The grasses of Ialibu are not the soft, domesticated grasses of American suburbia. Instead, they are aggressive in their response to human intrusion. Even a brief venture off the beaten track leaves one scratched and bleeding, and susceptible to the infections and ulcers that certainly will follow. Humans are not welcome here.

One is never certain whether what is underfoot is solid or liquid. Straying from the brown, time-worn walking paths becomes an exercise akin to negotiating a natural mine field. Each step displaces water in volumes that betray foot size. Some steps lead to even greater excitement, as thick gray mud grips one's leg to the knee in a frantic attempt to hold its human prey, as if the earth might reduce its hunger with human protein. And in this muck live migratory microscopic beasts excited at the prospect of shifting residence from the cold water to a warm human body, through a beckoning fissure in the skin.

Scattered throughout this spongy carpet are islands of even deeper green. Islands of trees, whose shadows provide shade from the occasional morning sunshine and whose leafy canopy provides protection from the battering administered by the perpetual afternoon rains, are home to the Imbi. Nestled among these trees are the houses to which the Imbi retire each evening to seek refuge from their harsh environment, from their enemies, from their ghosts, and from themselves.

Also scattered across this carpet are rocks and small hills resting miles from their birthplaces. They came to rest not as a result of being transported by water or rolling downhill in surrender to the demands of gravity. Their presence is something of a cosmic miracle, and it permits the Imbi and others to live where life might otherwise be impossible.

On the north of the basin stands Mount Giluwe. It rises to a majestic height of nearly fifteen thousand feet above the sea, a fact the Imbi do not know. More impressive to them is that Mount Giluwe stands eight thousand feet above the saturated, flat basin on which Imbi villages float, only inches above their own sea level. Like an ancient man, this ancient mountain is bald and its face is scarred with

Mount Giluwe, as seen across the Ialibu Basin from the summit of Mount Ialibu

the wrinkles of time. The Imbi know that Giluwe is like a man in more ways than physical appearance alone. Giluwe is alternately greedy, jealous, aggressive, mischievous, temperamental, and forgiving.

On the southern edge of the basin stands Mount Ialibu. Younger than Giluwe, Ialibu stands straighter, but not as tall. At eleven thousand feet he is an adolescent. But in his youth he is stronger than Giluwe. The adventurous who seek the view from atop the two mountains find the physical exertion required to reach the two summits is inversely proportional to the vertical distances travelled. Like his uncle to the north, Ialibu is more than a mountain. He is also greedy, jealous, aggressive, mischievous, temperamental, and forgiving.

Like insects that are no more than an annoyance to the Imbi, people are only an annoyance to Giluwe and Ialibu. And like humans who are jealous of one another, Giluwe and Ialibu do not get along. They fight. Like western oil companies who benefit from a reasonable level of discord among OPEC members, the Imbi and their neighbors have benefited from the tension and occasional outbreaks of violence between their giant neighbors.

A long time ago, Giluwe and Ialibu became angry with one another. Tobil, who knew the story best, told it to me. In their anger the mountains yelled at one another and hurled insults. Only the mountains know why they fought. Their problems are not the domain of humans, who were not present at the onset of the Giluwe-Ialibu feud. Humans are best served merely by ducking their heads and staying out of the way. The shouting continued for a very long time. The two mountains are only a few miles apart, but since they are unable to walk they must vent their anger from a distance.

As with men, the conflict between Giluwe and Ialibu escalated. Hurling insults may have been gratifying at first, but it became increasingly unfulfilling. The two giants began to hurl rocks instead of words. But the combatants were far apart, and lacked the strength to reach one another with their missiles. As a result, they fell short in their attempts to hurl themselves onto each other. This is no mere figure of speech, Tobil noted. As each picked a rock from his flank to hurl at the other, he was thwarted by gravity. Each missile was pulled to earth on the moist carpet between them. One failed attempt at vengeance became Koraipe, a modest lump that sits in the center of the basin. It is a chunk of Giluwe that he hurled at Ialibu, at whose feet it came to rest. Other, smaller, mountain body parts lay strewn across the basin, monuments to geological aggression. Some rocks, so heavy that they crashed through the fragile surface of the basin, created depressions that filled instantly with water that reflects the gaze of the sky. The new lakes and ponds created a habitat for fish, frogs, and other aquatic life. The seemingly floating lumps of hard earth provided purchase for plants that refused to grow in the soggy basin.

Like their human neighbors, Giluwe and Ialibu came to the realization that their violence was self-destructive. The lumps and depressions between them comprised the cemetery for their war dead, each grave literally a piece of the two warriors. One day they agreed to a formula for peace. They agreed to become friends again and to set aside their disagreements, precursors to German reunification and Arab-Israeli peace talks. The two agreed to a montane state dinner to celebrate peace. In the manner of their human neighbors, the two mountains agreed to slaughter pigs and share the meat. But also like their human neighbors, they became distrustful of one another's commitment to the cause of peace, and hostilities resumed. Following this renewed violence, the two again agreed to discuss peace. This time the preparations went smoothly. Each delivered pigs and vegetables to Koraipe, where a feast would seal the peace. The leftovers provided seed stock for the humans who recently had come to live in the basin. New lands and new lakes were joined by new plants, and the conditions for sustained human habitation were assured.

But the immigrant Imbi came to know, as have many small nations in Europe and Asia, that life can be difficult in the shadows of giants. Giluwe and Ialibu seemed unable to resolve their grievances permanently. Periodic eruptions of violence continued, placing the Imbi and their neighbors at risk. The mountains hurled rocks, which crashed through Imbi roofs. They breathed fire, which set Imbi roofs ablaze. They exhaled dust clouds, which settled on gardens, killing crops. And they belched clouds of gas and smoke, which produced darkness and fear. More than once the Imbi became refugees from the conflicts of their giant neighbors.

Tobil's imagery aside, Giluwe and Ialibu are only rocks. More specifically they are volcanoes, both long dead. Anthropologists and geologists have succeeded in linking the two sciences so as to explain many cultural stories and myths by reference to actual geological events. In the process, New Guinea's "time of darkness" stories, which are so widespread, have become little more than clever cultural markers of physical events (Blong 1982). Western scientists find great satisfaction in having successfully replaced myth with fact. The Imbi do not share that elation. The deaths of spirits and deities are difficult to accept.

Several years after I first heard all these stories, I was working and living in the national capital of Papua New Guinea. Port Moresby is a great distance both physically and culturally from Ialibu and the Imbi. But that world is shrinking. One day as I was walking in a section of the city known as Boroko, I heard my Imbonggu name, Kondoli, followed by my Imbi-ized English name, Billio. I turned to see a smiling face from the past. Koiyabo, now a Catholic named Victor, was attending a vocational school in the Badili section of Port Moresby. We resumed our friendship, with him coming regularly to my house in Gerehu.

Victor insisted on helping my wife attempt the impossible. That is, the two sought to create a garden in the barren desert that is Port Moresby for nine months each year during the dry season. A far cry from the Ialibu Basin.

One day, as they worked in their pitiful plot, Victor carefully positioned a stone. He excitedly explained to Diane that the stone would grow larger in time. Welcome news, as surely nothing of the plant variety was destined to grow there. Recognizing the look of disbelief on her face, Victor hastened to point out that this was a village belief, and one he no longer shared with his less sophisticated Imbi brothers back home in Ialibu.

Victor's denial of life to the rock took me back to Tobil's house. Years before, I had sought to tweak Tobil's curiosity with references to volcanic processes. He smiled, as if he were observing a child fumbling with a simple truth. If Giluwe is nothing more than a volcano that cooks its insides and vomits them on us, he noted, there is little for him to teach our children about Imbi life. Like dead men who tell no tales, lifeless mountains offer no morals or instruction in the ways of social life. And, of course, as even Americans know, some rocks make wonderful paperweights, while others make trouble-free pets. Certain others proclaim values of love, devotion, trust, and remembrance. And a few exceptional ones possess the improbable power to fell giants.

7 / Wandering Imbi

The large, flat basin that sits at the feet of Giluwe and Ialibu, and between the two mountains, is home to several thousand Imbonggu. They live in clearly defined territories they guard jealously against incursion by neighbors and outsiders. It is unclear how people came to exist in the first place. The Imbi recount no cosmic myth relating the origins of the universe and its components. After all, until the very recent past the universe extended only to Giluwe in the north and to Ialibu in the south. Other boundaries are defined by neighbors who surround the Imbonggu. The Mendi live to the northwest, the Kewa to the west, and the Wiru to the south and southeast. To the southeast, on the opposite side of Mount Ialibu from the Imbonggu, the mountain's slopes plummet through extremely rough country, which is very sparsely populated. To the east and northeast, the Kaugel River provides another boundary. The people who live in the area of the Kaugel are generally accepted by the Imbi as more closely related to the Imbonggu than to the more easterly groups closer to the Wahgi Valley. Contact among the Imbonggu and their neighbors remains limited, as it apparently was in the past.

This small universe belongs to the Imbonggu, a collection of smaller constituents such as the Imbi. It is not unique. The Imbonggu know of neighboring universes that are essentially identical in social terms, only the physical boundaries being different. The Imbonggu interact with all these neighboring universes through exchange, marriage, and warfare. Occasionally, groups like the Imbi actually migrate from one universe to another. Most stories that detail the histories of groups in the area relate exactly such migrations. As with individuals, larger groups come and go. Sometimes such arrivals and departures were the results of choice, more often the consequences of violence and warfare.

I was determined to learn the origin myth of the Imbi, the Imbonggu version of Genesis. But if there is an Imbonggu big bang theory, I never uncovered it. The rantings, ravings, and explosions of Giluwe and Ialibu were periodic expressions of emotion rather than analogs of the cataclysmic events that tend to characterize the explanatory models and origin myths of Western society. No big bang. No God creating man in his image. Only the most liberal interpretations of the stories I heard could be construed in such exciting terms. Rather, the physical world of the Imbonggu had always simply been there. The same was true of people, although humans in Imbonggu stories often transform their shapes at will from human to animal and from animal to human. Within that world, the Imbi were here one year, somewhere else the next.

If there is an Imbi founder, he is Puwi, son of Aiye. On the opposite side of Mount Ialibu from where Tona now sits, lived a man named Aiye. As Yombi and

Yama tell the story, Aiye lived in the eighth generation before those two old men. Each tells the story in similar general terms. But each tells the story from his own genealogical perspective, from Aiye to Yombi (or Yama) through a chain of father-son connections across the generations. Yombi recalls the story as he learned it in his youth from his father, Kuno. Physical evidence of the truth of the tale was contained in the skulls of Akipo, Yokop, Kondodl, Edlmongo, Puwi, and Aiye, which rested in skull houses built by the Imbi. Those physical remains no longer exist. Early Australian government officials, in league with Christian missionaries, destroyed the skulls, dozens of magical stones, and a host of other "heathen" objects. Colonial officers and missionaries wrought their destruction in their zeal to institute pacification and Christianity, respectively. But, as Yombi notes, though the skulls and skull houses are gone, they live on in his own skull, and he will pass that knowledge on to his sons and grandsons.

Aiye's village was at the base of Mount Ialibu on the opposite side of the mountain from where Nagop sits today. His son, Puwi, also lived there. But life was very difficult. Everyone became ill. Their stomachs were bloated, while their arms and legs shrunk and became very weak. No one knew the cause of this plague. One day a visitor arrived in this stricken village. He came from Piambil, an Imbonggu village in the Ialibu Basin. When he returned to his home, he took the deathly ill Puwi with him. In an effort to revive Puwi's health, this benefactor fed him and cared for him until he recovered.

One day Puwi went hunting in the bush. He took a hunting dog with him in hopes of capturing some possum. The area where he chose to hunt was unoccupied and heavily forested. The dog became attracted to a small tree. He stood at its base and barked repeatedly. The hunter assumed the dog had tracked a possum. When Puwi reached the tree, the dog was digging at its base. He chased the dog away, and continued digging in the ground at the foot of the tree. Puwi was certain that a possum must have excavated an underground lair. But after digging all the way around the tree, Puwi was forced to conclude that no possum lived there. Instead, two stones lived under the tree. Fearing their anger at destroying their house, Puwi built a new house for the two stones. He also built a new house for himself nearby. The modern village of Kuminge sits on the spot, named after the tree discovered by Puwi's hunting dog.

Puwi also built some gardens near his new house. He then returned to Piambil to tell his friend about these events. He named the two stones Keperia and Andoria. Puwi then returned to his father's village on the backside of Mount Ialibu and encouraged all his relatives who had survived the terrible disease to join him in his new village. Sensing the significance of the discovery of the two stones, they chose to follow him to their new home. Puwi's new village came to be known as Kuminge.

But the newfound prosperity of Kuminge was destined to be short-lived. A mile away, the Ango observed this incursion from atop Koraipe, a small hill rising from the soggy Ialibu Basin. The Ango had always considered the forested bush area discovered by Puwi to be theirs. Angered by this imperialistic intrusion, the Ango eventually attacked Kuminge and drove Puwi's descendants away. Some fled northward to the slopes of Giluwe, while others fled in the opposite direction, southward to Pangia.

Older men were willing informants concerning Imbi history.

Puwi's descendants settled into their new lives as refugees, and eventually became accepted in their new homelands. Disease had forced them to move to Ialibu. Violence had forced them to move again. Still more lay in store for these wanderers, however—white men. Sometime after the arrival of the first white men, the Imbi returned to Kuminge. They assumed that the new rules against fighting would protect them from the Ango. But the Imbi learned instead that white men were not to be trusted. The new colonial courts ruled that the Imbi held no claim to Kuminge and would have to leave. They were permitted to settle a short distance away. They established villages at Tona and Nagop, which they continue to occupy. Eight generations after the plague on Aiye's village, the wandering Imbi came to rest.

8 / What's in a Name?

Anthropologists have traditionally devoted much energy to the documentation of social organization among the people with whom they live and work. It provides an excellent vehicle for defining the content and relationships of the social universe. Unlike American society, and Western society generally, which seems bent on the goal of eliminating kinship in favor of social programs administered by governments and insurance companies, the Imbi cling to the belief that one's strength lies in the family and the larger kinship group. The axiom that blood is thicker than water is one of the few bits of Western wisdom the Imbi accept without reservation or the need for interpretation. In order to separate the blood from the water, my first task would be to conduct my own census. This would provide a structured activity within which I could meet everyone in the village and place them in sociological relationships to one another. It would also provide an opportunity to assess the potential skills of individuals as assistants and informants. Geoff Cowper kindly offered me the use of the official census books of the Local Government Council. These census books were used in the annual collection of the Council head tax. I thanked him for yet another kindness, tucked the books under my arm, and set off to do a very leisurely census. I even harbored fantasies of updating the books for Geoff, correcting errors, and so forth.

I informed Turi of my plan to visit each Imbi house, draw a map of the Nagop and Tona territories, and learn the names of every man, woman, and child. It was an excellent idea, he agreed. We would begin right away. Yombi's house was the obvious place to start. I found the page in the census book on which Yombi and his family were recorded, and we set to work. Australian patrol officers were many things, but they were not linguists. I found the names in the book seldom bore more than the slightest resemblance to the names as pronounced by their bearers. I had decided to write all my field notes such that all Imbonggu words were transcribed in the international phonetic notation system. Since the latter system contains approximately six times as many characters as the English alphabet, there would be no confusion as to how a written word was pronounced. Fine for me. Not so fine for the Council census books. The latter were written in English. As I would come to appreciate, that was not completely accurate. Actually, they were written in English filtered by Australian ears. There is a difference.

Yombi's was destined to be the first as well as the last household for which I would employ the Council census books. Turi assembled Yombi, his wife Alu, and their children Purul, Kanambo, Tongei, and Indipendo. Looking at the book I was surprised to see that Indipendo's name had been entered mistakenly as Nasil. I experienced a strange sense of satisfaction. I would indeed be able to help Geoff tidy up his census books. When I told Yombi of the erroneous entry for his youngest daughter, he expressed neither surprise nor concern. I explained it all in detail. To my confusion, he assured me that both names were correct. Indipendo was actually Nasil, but her name had been changed to commemorate the first celebration of National Day following her birth. Some people now called her Indipendo. Others continued to call her Nasil. Both were correct. Yombi used whichever name tumbled from his tongue first, like American parents with two children whom they constantly confuse, uttering the name of one when it is the other whose attention is sought. Life was simpler for Yombi. Whether he called for Indipendo or Nasil made no difference as she answered to both. We bid farewell to Yombi and his family, including Indipendo and Nasil.

Wareia's house was next. We were joined by Wareia, his wife Kelo, and their children. Whereas we had been left alone at Yombi's house, we were now joined by a small entourage of onlookers who apparently lacked anything better to do. I was unable to locate Wareia's name in the census book. Nor could I find Kelo. I set the census book aside. I would complete my own census forms. I decided to dispense with worrying about entering ages. I would merely do a census of names, create my map, and worry about a complete census later. I entered Wareia's name. Almost as an afterthought I remembered Yombi's explanation of the meaning of Indipendo and his reason for bestowing the name on his daughter. In a flash of inspiration, I asked Wareia what his name meant, and why his father had given it to him. The crowd that surrounded us collapsed in laughter. Wareia's head slumped sheepishly toward his chest. Men, women, and children all commenced to yell "Wareia!" seemingly at the top of their lungs, and then to lapse into hysterical laughter. Obviously, something was interesting about poor, embarrassed Wareia's name. When calm was restored, partly from exhaustion and partly from Turi's persistent demands, Wareia began to explain his name. I learned that Imbonggu do not normally name children at birth. In fact, to do so entails rather serious risks during the first few months of a fragile life. The innocent uttering of a name may attract the attention of spirits. Some of those spirits are likely to be hostile and may cause harm to the person whose name is spoken. Since children are vulnerable to a multitude of threats from a multitude of directions, the refusal to bestow a name on newborns is a pragmatic concession to spirits. By refraining from assigning a name to vulnerable newborns, the risk of harm by spirits can be mitigated to some extent. At Wareia's birth, his father was busy working near the house. Not so close as to be polluted by the birth process, but close enough to be apprised of progress. When he was informed that he was the father of a son, he went racing across several gardens exclaiming to all within earshot that his son was a "man." One of the many Imbonggu words designating man is *wareia*. Older people recall with hilarity the spectacle of Wareia's father running across the fields screaming, "Man! Man!" Were enemy raiders approaching the village? Were equally frightening white men venturing back? What was this man's problem? What had induced his obvious lunacy? When Wareia's father regained his calm and explained that his wife had given birth to a son, the news was a decided anticlimax. Shaking their heads in disbelief, people returned to what they had been doing prior to the interruption. Most were unaware that not only had they been present at the birth of a boy, but they had been witness to his accidental naming, and the birth of something of a legend.

Learning the meanings of Imbonggu names was itself a fascinating exercise (Wormsley 1981). Names were selected with care and deliberation. A name invariably served a purpose. By contrast, American names seldom indicate anything beyond personal taste or a sense of what others will find attractive in a name. An Imbonggu name may reflect characteristics of the child or a parent or close relative at the time of the child's birth. Thus Mopune means a beautiful young woman, which Mopune was. Globeke means to hide. He was born while his mother was still in hiding, having eloped with Globeke's father. The physical environment may inspire a name. Wakea was named for the leaves of a gingerlike plant that grew near his father's house. The contemporary social environment may generate a name. Garu means finished, which aptly described the fortunes of his father's clan at the time of Garu's birth. All the men of the clan had been killed or run off their land in recent fighting.

Events and travels also contribute to the pool of names as they are applied to Imbonggu children. Napile was so named because at the moment of her birth her father was away in the valley of the Nebilyer River arranging a large distribution of valuable shells. Kiapo was named for the arrival of Australian patrol officers, colonial officials known as *kiaps*. Chance plays its role as well. Kabame was named for the moss that covers a region of Mount Ialibu. The area is inhabited by dangerous spirits. When she was born, her father found his attention inexplicably drawn to that region. Since the arrival of foreigners in the Imbonggu territory, names have been borrowed from the newcomers. The Imbonggu reason that such names are associated with wealth and material items, and to possess the name may eventually result in other benefits. So Rusi derives from Ruth, Iote from Joseph, and Kote from court (in the legal sense). Debini, who could not sing a note, was named for a country and western singer (Skeeter Davis) after the latter was heard one evening via shortwave transmission on Radio Australia. Imbonggu also hold the belief that a name may produce a situation similar or identical to the one from which it was derived. Thus Pera named his daughter Mone, in the hope that she would bring him a large bride price (in cash money) upon her marriage.

Other considerations are to be taken into account when selecting a name. Unlike Americans who often apply the names of dead relatives, Imbi steadfastly refuse to use the names of the recently deceased. Such names may not be reassigned for years. A generation may pass before the name is employed within the family line of the deceased. Further, when someone dies, every surviving close relative bearing the same name must give it up and take a new one. Depending on the death rate and the laws of chance, every Imbonggu could go through several name changes as names become taboo following deaths. Death is not the only reason for changing a name, however. Someone may simply feel like a change, and announce that from here on he or she will be known by a new name. The number of names simultaneously associated with an individual was also fascinating. Most Americans inherit a surname over which we have little or no control. In addition, we are given other names, normally two. The "middle name" is of little practical value beyond distinguishing us from all the others who might bear the same surname and given first name. Middle names are also helpful in cases where they are more appealing than the first name. We may be addressed by several variants of those given names, but almost never would we refer to George Thomas Smith as "William." More

Napile, named after the Nebilyer River

likely he would be George, Thomas, Georgie, Tom, Tommy, G.T., or something close to one of those. He might even be known as Smitty, Bud, Lumpy, or some incomprehensible nickname among his particularly close friends. But Imbonggu naming patterns provided a smorgasbord of possibilities. As an individual Imbi goes through life changing his or her name at will, the previous names continue to be employed by anyone who prefers them, with the exception of those names prohibited from use following a death. Some collections of people might know him only by one name, others by many names they might employ interchangeably.

The creation of alias names is mandatory for men. Americans associate an alias with a Wanted poster on the bulletin board at the post office. But an Imbonggu male must assume an alias each time he becomes involved in an in-law relationship. Each time he marries, or each time he gains brothers-in-law following the marriage of a sister, he and his new brothers-in-law must assume aliases for use between themselves. They may not address one another except through the use of those aliases. So in addition to several given names and selected names, a man may be known by several alias names. The more wives and married sisters he has, the more aliases he will possess. These names are normally constructed along the lines of puns. If a man is named for a tree, he may be given an alias meaning a type of bush or grass.

I was totally taken with the meanings of names. The exercise of recording them became a trek through Imbonggu history, geography, botany, medicine, politics, even whimsy. The inevitable occurred one night as several people were crowded around my hearth. Yombi asked what my full name was. He knew of the tradition of *masta* (a Neo-Melanesian word used to refer to white men) normally having three names. Wormsley was first, it being my father's family name. Having just read a volume on the ancient roads of England, I explained that my father's family may have been named for such a road (a ley), probably having lived along such a track. Or my family might have resided historically in an area of Herefordshire, England, known as Wormsley. Some of my specific facts may have been incorrect, but the reasoning was plausible to the Imbi. Having had no children, and therefore no reason to purchase that American standard *500 Favorite Names* at the supermarket checkout counter, I was at a loss for William and Edward. I explained that William was a great warrior who had conquered England thirty or forty generations ago. Edward was a king who ruled England some generations later. Both names were quite commonly given to boys in America.

What about Bill? As every anthropologist knows, it takes someone like an Imbi informant to point out conclusively that we usually know a great deal more about their culture than about our own. I had no idea how William becomes Bill. But that answer was treated with obvious skepticism. How could a mature adult be unaware of the meaning and etymology of his name? It seemed clear to me that there was a great deal of doubt and the sense that I was withholding information. Given Imbonggu acceptance of the power of names, was I selfishly withholding potentially powerful knowledge? Fearing that I was becoming guilty of being an uninformative informant, I decided to create an instructional tall tale of the sort both Americans and Imbonggu rely on so heavily. The purpose of such tales is not to lie in the sense of obscuring or denying the truth. Rather, it is to pass on useful cultural information where no true episode or anecdote is available for that purpose. With the caveat that I did not know why I had been given my name, I could explain what the word itself means to Americans. In effect, I created a "just so" story accounting for my name. Kipling had accounted for the camel's hump, the leopard's spots, and other phenomena by means of his famous "just so stories." The Imbonggu told comparable stories to account for a variety of situations. Wareia had told me the story of how female genitalia came to be. Tobil told me how the feuding between Ialibu and Giluwe created the Ialibu Basin. Nabene told me the story of how two boys had been transformed into birds. All mothers and fathers were adept at creating stories urging children to demonstrate desired behavior. Such stories were often based on half-truths and simple falsehoods employed in the cause of good. Tremendous value is placed on the ability to recount traditional tales as well as to create new ones as situations demand. A truly skilled storyteller can hold an Imbonggu audience spellbound. I speak from experience. One such creative story included a most bizarre character, none other than a cannibalistic anthropologist (see Chapter 13).

As for Billio, encouraged by the questions, comments, and laughter of my audience, I wove a story in which my parents named me William at birth. That name was entered on all my official papers. I stayed in the hospital with my mother for several days. I explained that in America you must pay for everything. So when it was time to leave the hospital, my father was presented with a statement of the costs. So many dollars for use of the bed by my mother, more dollars for the use of a crib by me, money for the doctor, money for the nurses, and so on. That demand for money, I explained, is the bill. Unless my father paid the bill, I would not be allowed to leave the hospital with my parents. The bill was so expensive that my father had feared he could not pay it. Later, he gave me my alias (Bill) so he would not forget how much I had cost him.

My audience was impressed. It was agreed that this was indeed a very fine story. But was it true that people had to pay large sums of money to receive hospital care in America? As so often happened around my hearth, this story became just another springboard for a discussion of life in the world's foremost capitalist democracy. It also produced a vocabulary lesson of potential practical value in the event that I require an alias at some time in the future. The few Imbi who had learned a smattering of English at the Catholic primary school seven miles away, or the few who knew Neo-Melanesian through some other means, had not encountered the word *bill*. Their teachers, invariably Australian, employed other words, such as docket, check, receipt, or invoice. We discussed them all in detail. Arume noted that if I married Peni, he could not call me Bill. He would call me Invoice. If I married Mare, Pera would call me Docket. And on it went to the accompaniment of raucous laughter. For the time being, until these marriages occurred, I would remain Billi or Billio, the expensive baby from America.

There was another interesting aspect of Imbonggu names. Adult women seldom shared in them. Women had names, of course, but they were often the names of foreigners and enemies, and those names seldom became the names of young girls born in Imbi villages. The reason for this seemingly bizarre situation was one of the simplest explanations of any among the fascinating puzzles I encountered while living with the Imbonggu. The fact of the matter was that all the married women among the Imbi were indeed foreigners. And they were enemies, or at least the daughters and sisters of enemies. Married at fifteen, living until age sixty, they would spend three-quarters of their lifetimes as outsiders, just passing through, looking in. They brought their foreign names with them, constant reminders of their immigrant status. The girls born in Imbonggu villages eventually married and often took their names to non-Imbonggu villages where they would spend their lives as foreigners.

9 / Sexes at War

One of the more immediately discernible facts of highlands culture is that social groups are small and fiercely autonomous. The accounts of the earliest Australian colonial officers indicate that this has been the case for a long time. Oral histories suggest that this may have been true as long as people have lived in New Guinea. There is something of a siege mentality among highlanders, a sense that they are surrounded by enemies bent on their elimination. Fear and paranoia dominate the inventory of emotions and set the tone for intergroup and interpersonal relations.

Groups of men, related by ties of shared descent through males, sit sprinkled across the highlands. These patrilineal societies are separated by mountain ridges, river valleys, or the wasted no-man's-lands created by the wars they fight. In the Eastern Highlands, such war is largely a thing of the past. At the other end of the spectrum lies Enga, where war is of the present. Sadly for the Enga, it is probably also the way of the future. I spent three and a half years among the Enga studying warfare. Its toll on their lives is beyond comprehension. Its toll on me was great enough that to this day I find it hard to think positively of my time there. My research was fascinating, but I cannot recall Enga smiles.

The Ialibu Basin, in the Southern Highlands, occupies a middle ground on this historical continuum of tribal warfare in the highlands of New Guinea. War is a recent enough way of life that old men recall their exploits vividly. But it is receding. The younger generation of men seeks success on the battlefields of sexual conquest and the modern job market. But if warfare has split the scene in Ialibu, the fear and suspicion that accompany the threat of violence remain facts of everyday experience. Men occasionally grab their bows and arrows and set off to taunt similarly armed enemies. Fortunately, the groups more often fire insults and rocks than arrows at one another.

Fear and distrust continue to define intergroup relations for the Imbi. When I went walking in other clan territories, Imbi invariably warned me against accepting food that would probably contain poison. Neighbors are threats to one's life and health. Neighbors are a constant source of conflict. Neighbors are enemies in Imbonggu eyes. Neighbors are to be done unto first, before they can do unto. Neighbors serve only one or two possible positive purposes. One of those is their participation in exchange systems. The other is the provision of wives. And in the minds of Imbonggu men that is a very mixed blessing. Make no mistake about it. Men want it both ways. They want the strengths women potentially provide, but without the threats that are equally part of the package.

Women are far less dominant players than men in the scripts that define their lives. Most marriages among the Imbonggu continue to be arranged with little or no prior participation by the young women. Fathers trek the countryside seeking to arrange the most advantageous marriages for their daughters. A young woman may be the currency with which a debt is paid off. More likely she will be the currency with which a debt is created. When she is married, her new husband and his kinsmen will make a previously negotiated payment to her father. Before the arrival of colonial culture, that payment was in the form of pigs, shells, and cassowaries. The shells were of immense value because they were imported from the coastal villages along the Gulf of Papua via long and winding trade routes involving several trading partners. Cassowaries are large birds, emu-like in appearance. They are famous for their intensely foul disposition. Their objection to capture is so violently communicated that men hunt them only as chicks, capturing them in traps. The bird then lives its life in a shelter that is both house and cage. One day, when the cassowary is as tall as its keeper, after having spent most of its life standing up and sitting down, much like a steer in a Nebraska feed lot, it will stick its head through its cage to eat. Greeted by a violent neck-breaking twist at its master's hands, it will die without knowing that it is part of the payment for an Imbonggu bride. Few cassowaries remain in the Ialibu region today.

In the modern Imbi world, marriage payments invariably contain sums of money. As mentioned earlier, the national currency of Papua New Guinea is the kina and the toea. One hundred toea equal one kina. Toea was a traditional valuable among some of the islanders living on the large island of New Britain, to the east of the main island of New Guinea. Kina were the pearl shells that made their way to the highlands, where coastal garbage became the wealth of mountainous realms. Optimistic fathers invariably seek enormous payments and trumpet the virtues of their available daughters accordingly. But women being everywhere, and their individual virtues being of little or no significance to the Imbi, the hope for payment of several dozen pigs and several thousand kina routinely dwindles to about a dozen pigs of varying size and two or three hundred kina. These payments are hotly debated, and negotiations may be carried on for months. But eventually a marriage is arranged, usually sooner rather than later. Most Imbonggu girls are married by their seventeenth birthday, although the Imbonggu pay no attention to such precise temporal markers.

Ironically, such payments have become the subject of even more heated debate among anthropologists than among the people around the world who arrange them. For most of its existence, the vast body of anthropological knowledge has included the concept of brideprice. The wealth paid at the marriage of an Imbonggu woman would have been described as such without comment, at least until recently. But like Western society at large, anthropologists find themselves engaged in a range of revisionist debates attacking the accepted wisdom of orthodox anthropological theory. One of the more successful revisionist attacks has been waged against the concept of brideprice. The argument is both seductive and revealing of its origins. It goes like this: Women are not property, and cannot be bought and sold. Men (like the Imbonggu) are not actually purchasing a wife as the word "price" implies. Rather, the man's and woman's families are entering a complex and lifelong series of economic exchanges. There is a better designation for such payments: bridewealth.

So what are we to make of the change in terminology from brideprice to bridewealth? Does it reflect a change in the cultural and social behavior described and analyzed? Clearly not. Does it reflect the intrusive dominance of the shared cultural beliefs and values of anthropologists themselves? One can only hope not. After all, if anthropology is about anthropologists, then Deloria (1969) was correct in stating that anthropologists have done more harm than good to the people they study. Does such revisionism betray a more subtle ethnocentrism? In other words, rather than simply saying that another's cultural behavior is wrong as an unschooled tourist might do, are anthropologists occasionally guilty of producing inaccurate but more appealing descriptions that are at variance with reality? Put bluntly, are we sometimes guilty of describing what we wish were the case rather than a reality that may be inconsistent with our own values?

Imbonggu men, even Imbonggu women, know generally who will marry whom. The who and whom in this case apply to groups of people rather than individuals. The latter are in a sense interchangeable game pieces. But no one questions the game to which they belong. The issue is more often simply which seventeen-year-old girl will be put into play at a given time. Fathers seek to initiate the process early enough that prospective grooms (and their male relatives who will be contributing to the payment) can be played against one another to maximum advantage. This is bargaining. The best offer will likely secure the young woman as a wife.

That is not to suggest that the young woman is totally powerless, however. She still must agree, but it is exceptionally rare that she would reject her father's choice. Far more often, she makes it clear to him at the outset if one of his nominations is unacceptable to her. Most fathers do not waste their time on a match that will not be acceptable to a daughter. In this sense, she is much like the veteran major league baseball player who is entitled to determine his own list of teams he will agree to be transferred to in return for another player or cash. The father is much like the owner of the player's current team. He seeks to pit the acceptable teams against one another in an effort to get the best terms. The father of the prospective groom is much like the owner of one of those acceptable baseball teams. He seeks to obtain one of the players being offered to him by several other teams, each of those players having already given consent for a deal to be made. He seeks the player/bride who will fill most of his needs for the fewest dollars/pigs. The best analogy for Imbonggu marriage and brideprice may lie not in political theories of alliance or female autonomy, but in the movement of free agents in baseball. In that system players who enjoy considerable autonomy are nonetheless traded, dealt, sold, and acquired.

So, do the men of Tona pay brideprice or bridewealth when they marry? Trite as it may sound, the Imbonggu do what the Imbonggu do, and it probably is neither bridewealth nor brideprice in any pure sense. I retain the usage of brideprice in this account primarily due to its historically widespread application in highlands ethnography. Since its meaning, connotations, and even shortcomings are well-known to anthropologists, little analytical confusion results from use of the term. A second reason I employ it is that in cases where highlanders themselves use English to refer to the activity, they employ the term *brideprice* without exception or reservation.

It must be noted, however, that the Imbonggu are uninterested in debates about brideprice versus bridewealth. Nor do they distinguish between marriage as a means of creating or solidifying political and economic alliances and marriage as a means of maximizing economic cooperation within the domestic unit. They marry for either reason, and sometimes both. There is no more functional or secure avenue than marriage to achieve either goal. While wives are not wealth, they both symbolize it and generate it. While wives need not be obtained for the express purpose of facilitating the transfer of wealth among men, they nevertheless facilitate such exchange. These two considerations are likely to be far more crucial to older and more established men with aggressive political ambitions. For example, an Enga candidate once sought my advice as to where his eighth wife should come from. He had only enough assets to obtain one wife, but had been unable to narrow his choice down to one of two districts crucial to his election chances. Such are the ugly choices confronting the powerful or those who seek to be. Other men, particularly those who remain bachelors, face far less complicated decisions. Such youthful Imbi men obtain wives because there are certain roles in life for which women are the appropriate performers. In the Imbonggu scheme of things it is women who should do the bulk of the work associated with gardening, pig raising, and child rearing. An anthropological great named Ian Hogbin (1970) wrote a book with a most intriguing title, *The Island of Menstruating Men*. Catchy, but an idea that baffled Imbonggu, both male and female. My male Imbi friends merely chuckled at the oxymoron, suggesting that possibly I had misread it. Certainly what I had described to them was mere foolishness. Women menstruate, women become pregnant, and women give birth to children, they assured me. Women also tend gardens and pigs. So men must have wives.

As such topics of conversation became less embarrassing for the Imbi to discuss with me, they admitted that whereas children were necessary, they were hardly the only reason to engage in sex. Sex is fun. It carries risks, of course, because women are very dangerous creatures. In a view of intercourse with a tinge of the concept of limited good, Imbonggu men believe that semen both symbolizes and contains one's spiritual and physical essence. It can be both built up and depleted. Time and abstinence build it up. Sexual intercourse depletes it by passing it to a woman. If she turns it into a child, a man can feel pride and satisfaction. He can also feel a sense of security, as children are a sort of insurance against the poverty of old age. But if a woman merely allows his semen to spill from her body, then his essence has been wasted. He has been robbed, his strength sapped somewhat. Thus men limit their sexual activity as a form of self-defense, a sort of preventive health care.

But there is a more constraining reason why unmarried men abstain from sex. Until they are married, few, if any, women are available to them. It is decidedly wrong and unthinkable to have sex with girls and women born into one's own kin network. Such incest never occurs. The only women available in the safety of one's home territory who are not relatives, and thereby prohibited by the rules of incest from being sexual partners, are the wives of one's male relatives. Sex with such women is not necessarily incest, but it is frowned on generally by the husbands. Young men who have sex with a married woman may be killed by the husband. No one will object to the correctness of the cuckolded husband's action. Most often the youth will receive an emphatic beating, forfeit a hefty fine, and endure a painful dose of public humiliation in the bargain. So wives are necessary at a more basic level, not merely to perform specific economic tasks, but to satisfy a man's sexual urges as well.

Homosexuality is unthinkable to the Imbonggu. Even in the ancient male initiation practices, long terminated by Western influences, homosexual male intercourse was not practiced. To Imbi men I described the practice of ritual homosexuality among the Kaluli (Schieffelin 1976:122). Much of the region bordering the central highlands on the south is home to many groups that practice ritual homosexuality in secret male cults (Herdt 1987:101-169). Older men initiate younger men into the ways of society. They also augment the physical development of young boys by periodically injecting them with semen. This account was followed by a thundering silence in which Imbi men looked at me in utter disbelief and revulsion. Imbonggu men emphatically state their preference for women.

Women pose a variety of threats to men, however. Most obvious is the threat to physical and spiritual well-being through the act of intercourse. To the extent that men can control their own sexual impulses, they can mitigate this particular threat. But women pose another threat that is sexual in nature. Both the normal vaginal secretions of women and the blood expelled during menstrual periods threaten the health of men. To come into contact with these substances may cause men to become ill. They will gradually shrivel and waste away until rescued from their torment by inevitable death. This more general threat demands more than mere sexual abstinence. In a very real sense, the mere presence of women constitutes a threat. The two most obvious manifestations of these beliefs and fears are widespread residential segregation and a pervasive antagonism between the sexes (Langness 1967; Meggitt 1964).

I once witnessed a young woman being beaten severely by her angry husband. The episode provides vivid testimony to the depth of feeling manifest in such sexual antagonism. The man had placed his axe next to him on the grass as he sat on the ground to talk with several other men. His wife walked past, engaged in conversation with a second woman. Unaware, she stepped over his axe as she walked. She did not step on it, merely over it. Her husband flew into a rage. He screamed at her and slapped her several times. He picked up his axe and threatened to strike her with it. Thoroughly frightened and humiliated, she slunk away. He threw his axe to the ground in disgust. Some time later, he walked away, leaving his axe on the ground. He returned with a piece of wood from which he began to fashion a new handle to replace the polluted one.

The poor woman who stepped over her husband's axe did so accidentally en route from her house to one of her gardens. Her husband's axe happened to be between her origin and destination. Her bad luck. Until recently, Imbonggu husbands did not reside under the same roof with their wives. Increasingly there are exceptions as modern individuals become involved with the various Christian missions operating in the region. But even among this enlightened category separate houses for a man and his wives remain a reality. Wives and daughters continue to spend considerable time sleeping in their own houses, separate from their husbands and fathers. The wife's house is usually located some distance off the perimeter of the village, nestled among the low woman-made mounds incubating the family sweet potato crop. Occasionally her house may sit just off a path in a sea of tall grass, invisible to the unfamiliar passerby. In those marriages in which residential separation continues to be observed, except in rare circumstances, a wife will not enter her husband's house, nor will he enter hers. She will share her house with all her young children and her older daughters. At age ten or so, her sons will increasingly spend their nights with their father or his brothers, the two being designated by the same kinship term.

A wife's house may be home to others, such as another of her husband's wives if he has more than one. Depending on a variety of concerns, a husband may build separate houses for his wives. One of the dominant factors in this decision is the number of pigs for which each wife assumes quasi-parental responsibility. Pigs usually share the house of their human mother. Thus, for men who have more than one wife, the number of pigs as much as the number of wives determines how many houses he must construct and maintain for them.

Such are the parameters of male-female interaction among the Imbonggu. Men spend much of their time plotting the disposition of their women and their pigs. They must make decisions about when and to whom a daughter will become another man's wife. They must decide when it is both desirable and feasible to obtain a wife who will prepare gardens and shepherd a pig herd. They must decide about the wisdom and feasibility of disposing of some of the pig herd to obtain an additional wife. The woman's decisions are more limited to the specific issue of whom, with a minor influence over where (that is, which clan) and when. She will spend much of her time on her knees working in the garden to produce the food for her family and her pig herd. She will do so as a wife in what amounts to a foreign society in which she is perpetually a stranger. These separate male and female orbits occasionally intersect, and a risky sexual encounter or a heated domestic dispute may break the worldly monotony.

10 / Take My Daughter, Please!

Imbonggu men accept that women are basically quite dangerous to their physical and spiritual well-being. At the same time, all men accept that women are equally essential to their social and political well-being. Bachelors and spinsters are virtually unknown to the Imbi. For a person never to marry demands that he or she be universally recognized as severely handicapped, either physically or intellectually. All normal people marry. Most men aspire to have more than one wife, possibly several. Wives sharing the same husband occasionally experience some jealousy at the thought of sharing material wealth and attention. At the same time, they appreciate the advantages of sharing the labor requirement necessary to maintain a human family and pig herd.

Men seek the economic and political advantages of several wives, specifically the possibility of enlarging the pig herd that does so much to define a man's status. Men also appreciate the enhanced position of power that may come from marrying the daughters of politically important men in the larger Imbonggu universe. At the same time, men must deal with the inevitable jealousies among wives as well as the threat of their adulterous liaisons with other men, primarily younger unmarried men. Such adultery may proceed to the point where it becomes both a public embarrassment and a political liability if a man comes to be seen as one who cannot control his wives' behavior. Men must balance all these issues in deciding when to marry, how often to marry, whom to marry, and so forth.

Marriage is not merely a matter of a man seeking wives, however. Marriage is also a matter of another man seeking to arrange a marriage for his daughter. Certainly, in traditional patterns prior to foreign intervention, marriages were negotiated by the fathers of the future husband and wife. The latter parties were normally consulted prior to those parental negotiations. Sons might reject a woman if she were known to be lazy, disagreeable, or sexually promiscuous. Daughters might reject men who were known to be abusive in their treatment of women. Both sons and daughters tended to exercise limited rights of refusal, however, rather than unlimited rights of choice in proposing future spouses. There has been some recent change in these areas. Many children now attend regional schools where they meet their own potential spouses. As they observe foreign teachers, administrators, missionaries, and businesspeople, they come to accept the attractiveness of Western notions of romantic love and personal selection of marriage partners. Predictably, fathers see such changes as threatening illustrations of the sort of willfulness that results from the intrusion of foreign ideas into Imbonggu society, especially among the young, who are often described by their elders as *bikhet*. Individuals must balance all these factors when they reach the points in their lives when marriage becomes a matter to be addressed.

Older men continue to seek to arrange the marriage of their daughters to the men of their choice. They grant minimal concern to the specific preferences of their daughters unless those preferences are expressed forcefully. Men seek sons-in-law who are related to significant political leaders or to men who are wealthy. Fathers hope to receive a significant payment of pigs and cash at the marriage of a daughter. A marriage may either create indebtedness with potential advantage in the future, or it may balance out a debt incurred in the past. In this context, marriage can be defined as an economic transaction principally for the immediate benefit of the two fathers and the future benefit of the new husband. By contrast, the young woman will leave the security of her home to come under the thumb of a demanding mother-in-law or co-wives. She will move to a village where she will be defined as a threatening foreigner, an enemy. She will spend much of the rest of her life on her knees in a garden harvesting the food for her family and for the pig herd that will permit her husband to ascend the ladders of political and economic success. It is often difficult to ascertain either immediate or future benefits from her perspective.

Most anthropologists understand the existence of all these factors and concerns, and their analysis of marriage and its resultant kinship networks is generally the most sophisticated aspect of their work. But marriage creates a fascinating contradiction for anthropologists in the field. One worthy of examination, though such examination seldom occurs. In methodological terms, anthropology relies heavily on the concept of participant observation. Without elaboration, what is implied is that the anthropologist does more than merely observe in a detached manner, as if he or she were no more than a fly on the wall. As anthropologists, we claim that we learn much by participating in the lives of the people we study. But there are understood, though seldom explicitly stated, limits on our participation. Bronislaw Malinowski, an anthropological pioneer in conducting actual field research, lived among the Trobriand Islanders. He sets out fairly concisely what an anthropologist must do to set the stage for successful field research (Malinowski 1922:6–24). He instructs future generations on the need to achieve as close contact with informants as possible, preferably by "camping right in their villages" (Malinowski 1922:6). Ironically, Malinowski appears to have done exactly that (camped, that is), as one of the photographs in his book (Plate I, facing p. 16) includes his tent surrounded by Trobriand houses! Recent generations have opted for structures built of local materials by local craftsmen. Modern anthropologists have shed the trappings of the colonial era. They should eat local foods rather than the tinned products of home. They should learn the language rather than rely solely on a translator. At the opposite end of this integration spectrum lie two monumental exceptions, however. Anthropologists apparently should not marry their informants or engage in sexual intercourse with them. Anthropologists prefer to erect a barrier between themselves and their informants in these areas and to operate on the assumption that neither participation nor abstinence on the part of the anthropologist has any impact on the conduct of research or the understanding and analysis of data. Most anthropologists fail even to mention in their public writings those experiences and issues that pertain to sex and gender. Exceptions are few (Good 1991; Rabinow 1977:59–69; Whitehead and Conaway 1986).

Years after his death, excerpts of Malinowski's field diaries were published (Malinowski 1967). Something of an uproar ensued as anthropologists were confronted with the disturbing evidence that a founding father, an icon, was also human. He was frequently on poor terms with his informants. He occasionally employed racial epithets to refer to them, even going so far as to invent a Polish word for that purpose (Stocking 1983:102*n*). He repeatedly wrote of his intense loneliness. Because his fiancée lived in Melbourne, he suffered debilitating bouts of lovesickness as well. At one point he urged himself to repress his sexual urges, which on one occasion he indelicately refers to as "whoring impulses" (1967:181). What is most interesting is his obviously greater concern with the impact of such behavior on his relationship with his fiancée. But there exists little doubt that his field research was affected. After one such discussion he wrote in his diary, "As for ethnology: I see the life of the natives as utterly devoid of interest or importance, something as remote from me as the life of a dog" (1967:181). Clearly, Malinowski erected some barriers (or possibly merely allowed them to develop) between himself and Trobrianders. One of the key factors in the erection of those barriers was gender. Malinowski clearly underwent a frequently debilitating struggle to balance his own gender definitions, those of his fiancée and the society from which she came, still others held by expatriates living in the Trobriands, and those of the Trobrianders themselves.

I had read Malinowski's diary not to learn about him at a personal level for the sheer joy of watching an icon crumble. My purpose had been to understand the trials he faced in doing fieldwork, and possibly to glean some advice on how to deal with them should I find myself in his position. In that sense, the diary was as frightening as it was instructive. What would I do to avoid the pitfalls Malinowski confided in his diary? How would I seek to turn them to my advantage, or at least minimize their damage potential? Despite my repeated assertions that I was married and was not seeking an Imbonggu wife, men simply refused to accept this truth as immutable. Like the American boss who assumes that if he continues to ask his subordinate for a date she will ultimately relent, Imbi men continued to present me with marriage proposals. Men explained in detail the various merits of their daughters as well as the advantages I would gain by marrying one of them. Those explanations could only reflect Imbonggu values pertaining to the institution of marriage. As such, they deserve to be treated as valuable data that contribute to an understanding of Imbonggu cultural values and beliefs rather than as a mine field threatening the integrity of the relationship between researcher and informant. For many anthropologists, however, they raise the issue of the extent to which an anthropologist can intrude into his own data before he or she has intruded too far. In other words, can the anthropologist be part of the data he or she analyzes? Must we ignore the cases in which we become involved as if they are some kind of tainted data? Or should we somehow account for alterations in the shape and performance of events and activities in which we become involved? But it must also be recognized that the anthropologist often lacks the ability to control the research situation fully. Throughout my stay with the Imbi, whenever I walked anywhere with children, one would invariably walk ahead of me and assume the responsibility of alerting me to the locations of small piles of fresh *pekpek* strung along the path, usually deposited by pigs but occasionally by humans. Field research is much like life in many regards, and the anthropologist occasionally stumbles metaphorically into a pile of *pekpek*. One can only hope to make the best of such situations and emerge smelling like something else. For me, despite repeated and firm refusals, marriage proposals kept littering my path.

Pera stressed the fact that Mare was a very hard worker. Arume emphasized Peni's even disposition and obedience. Tobil reminded me that Kani was a virgin and obviously not given to sexual excess. Tiane was strong, unlike the white women at the government station seven miles away. Men also articulated the confusion generated by colonial experience. One daughter could read and write, and thereby could assist me in my work, whatever that was. Another could not read at all and thus would not be swayed by new ideas and become disrespectful. One had learned to like Western culture at school and would like to live in a house in town. Thus if I married her and accepted a job with the government, she would not run back to the village.

The characteristics of ideal wives were not the only factors to consider. Pera assured me that he was not overly concerned at my lack of pigs. He would accept a brideprice consisting solely of cash. Arume wanted a brideprice of pigs only. "It is too easy to lose money. And once it is lost, it cannot be easily regained," he explained. He proposed that he would accept a deferred payment. Since I had no pigs of my own, he would provide some to permit me to establish my own herd from which I would subsequently pay the brideprice. His strategy seemed akin to the concept of seller-financing in the American real estate market. It seemed clear that the men of the village would not accept "no" for an answer. As a result, I generated as much data as I observed in the areas of sex and marriage. But did the specific data that were the direct results of my physical presence merit diminished consideration, or even none at all, as a consequence?

11 / Banishing Peni

In recent years there has been a revolution in anthropology. The revolution is feminist in origin and is the inevitable outgrowth of the historical male dominance of the field. It is frequently argued that the predominance of male anthropologists has produced a biased body of knowledge in which the roles and contributions of women were accorded less attention and analysis than the comparable activities of men. Proclaiming that male anthropologists either could not or would not address issues of gender bias, feminist anthropologists set about correcting this situation, but in a sometimes disappointing and unsatisfying manner. Apparently beguiled by the possibility that two wrongs indeed make a right, contemporary anthropology has witnessed the emergence of a parade of volumes devoted to filling these gaps in the anthropological record with accounts that focus on women. A deluge of life histories of female informants has appeared, as well as volumes about the role of women in exchange and power relations. In many cases the new research is subject to much the same criticism as the earlier biased works it was designed to offset. It is as if some scholars sought to balance the scales by placing women on one half of the balance as a counterweight to the men firmly entrenched on the other. Of course, this situation mirrors the identical one confronting American society at large as we attempt to deal with race and sex bias. One has the unsettling suspicion that the real anthropological theory and understanding we seek probably rests somewhere in the middle. And like Lady Justice holding the pros and cons of her debate, one fears Lady Anthropology is also blindfolded, or possibly just blind. How would I avoid the same trap, the same error? Would I be able to deal with female informants? I would certainly make a conscious effort to be as unbiased as possible in an effort to avoid the charges of negligence and disinterest being hurled at my male anthropological ancestors.

One question remained, however. Would the Imbonggu cooperate? As in much of the world, the rule almost everywhere in Papua New Guinea is frightfully simple: men are in charge. Men may talk to women when they choose and in whatever manner they choose. Women should talk to men when invited or permitted. How would I fit into such an interaction pattern between the sexes? Female anthropologists suffer from the same problem in a structural sense. Ironically, what separates male and female anthropologists in their ability to address gender issues is often nothing more than their gender. But I was committed to making certain that I did not spend my time and effort disproportionately on Imbonggu men and their activities. It might be more difficult to interact with the women in Imbonggu villages, but I would not shrink from the task.

There were specific obstacles in dealing with women that I did not encounter with Imbonggu men. The most immediate concerned language and had nothing to do with gender in any direct sense. The adult women of the village often did not speak Imbonggu. They typically spoke any one of half a dozen other languages. Those who spoke Imbonggu presented additional difficulties, as they were normally quite young. More significant, they were unmarried and still living at home. When they became married they would live in a village where the men probably spoke some language other than Imbonggu. There was one other possibility, at least in the minds of several of the men of the village. One of these young women might become married to me. That would have been a problem only in the sense that one man would benefit a great deal while most others would forfeit some degree of access to me. Thus my interaction with younger, unmarried women was colored by the hopes of their fathers that I would become the wealthy son-in-law so many sought, but equally colored by the fear that I would not.

While the women of Tona and Nagop represented something of a human mine field for me, they also provided the means by which I learned a great deal about Imbonggu society and culture. Certain husbands were often suspicious of any time their wives spent with me. Men often inquired about my sex life. Their assumption was that I must be having sex, but with whom? Adultery was always a source of village gossip. To minimize the fallout on their various home fronts, married women preferred to meet with men (including me) in the company of other women or children. I preferred this also, as it increased the likelihood that someone would be available for translation when required.

Single women were often pressed into service by their fathers to bring me food and firewood. Such acts appeared designed as much to provide evidence of both the utility and availability of these dutiful daughters as to demonstrate Imbonggu kindness. The girls were discouraged from staying long at my house, however, in order to lessen the risk of any sexual activity that would reduce the marital value of any daughter I failed to marry.

Amidst this bewildering backdrop of conscious enticement on the one hand and suspected adultery on the other, I managed to develop several very close personal relationships with women. But none contained more pleasure or greater frustration than my interactions with Peni. Her name means "beautiful girl" and is more obviously apt than many Imbonggu names. We became fast friends. Much of what I know about Imbonggu was gained through her patient tutelage. Much of what she learned of life outside the village was extracted from me. Peni taught me the techniques used by women to prepare, maintain, and harvest their sweet potato gardens. She told me gossip and *tumbuna* (ancestors) stories around my hearth at night. As she became increasingly comfortable with me, she offered to accompany me to the local market one day where I could talk to women about their market activities. She sought to sell some excess sugar cane for a few spare coins to purchase some imported cotton yarn. As we walked the seven kilometers to the market ground, other travellers pelted Peni with a barrage of raucous hypotheses concerning her white male companion. To spare her further taunting, I did not accompany her into the market itself. My gesture must have been too little too late, however, for I later discovered she left the market early without earning enough money to purchase her yarn.

Anthropologist with Nabene, a key female informant

On another occasion, I made a trip to the town of Mount Hagen sixty miles to the northeast. I drove the small jeep of an American friend, Randy Bollig, who was a teacher at the nearby high school. Randy had several small errands to run and no time in which to carry them out. He offered me the use of his vehicle to go to Mount Hagen in return for conducting his business there. I invited Peni to go with me. She in turn asked her friend Mare, and the three of us set off to a city of fifteen thousand people, which was like another universe to two girls who had never been further from their homes than the market seven kilometers away.

We bounced along the highway for sixty miles in choking dust, the usual hail of small stones battering our windscreen. When we reached Mount Hagen, neither Peni nor Mare would venture from the safety of the vehicle. Neither girl dared set foot on the pavement that promised a totally new sensation for their naively rural feet. I bought them their first ice cream cones, which neither liked particularly. They disliked the sensation of the cold on their teeth, and pressed their lips against their teeth in an effort to recapture lost warmth. I drove to Mount Hagen's small Chinatown, a strip of closely bunched miniature department stores owned and operated by Chinese merchants. I explained that the stores contained a vast array of colored cotton yarns, lengths of imported *laplap* (printed cloth), and other items familiar to the girls. After much cajoling, and a steady stream of other women entering and exiting the store, Peni and Mare marshalled their courage. They wandered through the small store, oohing and ahing at the wealth contained in it. I bought Peni far too many skeins of yarn, and each of them a *laplap* for herself and another for her mother. In an effort to temper the inevitable suspicion, I bought several packets of tobacco to give to their fathers. In Neo-Melanesian, I was shamelessly guilty of attempting to *grisim* their fathers. In English, the word means to bribe, flatter, cajole, or otherwise sweet talk someone into behaving in a desired way.

The thing that most amazed Peni and Mare was the magical instant photo processing machine. Each had seen dozens of photographs I had taken and given to people in the village, but no one had ever given any thought to the basic question of how such photographs came into being. Everyone knew that I sent my films away somewhere and the pictures arrived some time later. But now the mystery, to the extent there had been one, was solved. Of course, the solution served only to create a multitude of questions. The two girls watched the machine from every conceivable angle. They pointed here and there to this sound and that movement, their brows furrowed in intense concentration, heads shaking in utter disbelief, totally oblivious to everything else in their expanding world. They talked about the machine during the entire drive home, and proceeded to offer up their own mime of the machine, plus simulated sounds, to an astonished audience around my hearth. I laughed at their blundering attempts to explain the machine to their puzzled audience, until it occurred to me that they understood the machine almost as thoroughly as I did!

As months passed, Peni lingered later and later at my house. She became the last to leave each night, as well as the first to arrive. She pressed me about America and Australia. Did I like teaching? Did I earn a lot of money like the Australians at the nearby government station? Their wives did not have to work at all. They simply went to Mount Hagen in a big truck and bought everything they needed. This was the sort of life she wanted. She did not want to marry a Papua New Guinean man who she feared would make her work in a garden all day and beat her when he became drunk. Most of all, she did not want to live in the village. She wanted a house in the European style, with stove, beds, mattresses, chairs, and water inside the house. I often felt guilty. I knew that Peni had been thinking such thoughts for a long time before I had arrived in the village. Still, I feared that by even discussing such matters with her I might be making a bad situation worse.

Peni had gone to a nearby Catholic mission elementary school several years before. In succeeding years, she had rejected every marriage agreement her father had painstakingly constructed. In fact, he was finding it increasingly difficult to find men willing to discuss the marriage of their sons to Peni, who was proving to be exceedingly uncooperative. This script was played out over and over during my stay in Tona. Peni vetoed marriage arrangements as rapidly as her father presented them to her. The last time I saw her before I returned to America after two years in the village, she informed me that she was going to run away or commit suicide. She would not marry a village man. By way of a postscript, after I left the village in 1977, Peni wrote to me in America for two years before her correspondence ceased. In 1985 I was returning to Enga after a trip to Lae. As I drove through the town of Goroka, approximately two hundred miles from Ialibu, I heard my name being yelled from a crowd of people at the side of the road. I pulled to a stop and stared dumbfounded as Peni ran toward my car. She had seen me drive past the market at which she did her daily shopping. I learned that she had married a high school teacher and was living in Goroka, in a European-style house.

Unknown to me at the time, certain men were jointly reaching the conclusion that Peni posed a significant threat to them. Specifically, they reasoned that she might eventually become my wife. Men with daughters old enough to marry preferred that I marry those daughters rather than Peni. Men without daughters preferred that I marry no one at all. Put bluntly, these positions were the logical products of a calculated assessment of the likelihood of continued access to the anthropologist's wealth. If I married a woman from the village, her father would have an advantageous position from which to lay claim to what was perceived as my vast wealth. Thus, as my relationship with Peni continued, I was forced to listen to ever more damning descriptions of her worthlessness and foul personality. But Peni and I remained friends. Our friendship, which I accepted as sincere and harmless, was becoming a major irritant for some of the men of the village, however. More than once, men told me that Peni should cease coming to my house. The situation finally came to a head following a most amazing chain of events.

Wareia, Yombi, Turi, and several other men were seated around my hearth early one morning. Men often stopped by my house on their various ways to collect firewood, to negotiate the marriage of a daughter, to attend sessions of the government court seven kilometers distant at Ialibu, or any of hundreds of other activities. Such visits were invariably accompanied by an invitation for me to pick up my camera and join them. Almost as often, they were accompanied by a request to provide some item essential to the completion of the task. Cigarettes were needed to smoke in the forest; money was required to pay the hire for a truck; or money was essential to pay an anticipated court fine. One of the men suddenly pointed at Wareia's leg as he sat cross-legged on my floor. "Some woman has left blood on Billio's floor!" All that followed transpired in the blink of an eye. To this day I remain firm in my recollection that Wareia actually levitated from the floor while he screamed in panic. Other men jumped to their feet, rearranging the bunches of leaves covering their backsides that had become disarrayed in the panicked movements. The young boys were sent from the house. The remaining men crowded around the telltale spot on the floor. Heated discussion was accompanied by frantic gestures. Poor Wareia glanced at his thigh in disgust, as if its amputation were imminent.

The conclusion was unanimous. The spot was blood. Worse, it was unquestionably a woman's menstrual blood. I didn't know whether to laugh or cry. That the spot was indeed blood offered not even the possibility of surprise. Half the men examining the spot on my floor had themselves limped into my house with gaping axe and knife wounds that they proceeded to unwrap for my viewing. I would then clean the wounds with Dettol, an Australian supermarket disinfectant, and cover them with clean strips of gauze. Later, I would clean my floor. On more than one occasion, wounds actually were inflicted by the floor itself. The floor was covered with plaited mats of a grass called *pitpit,* which was similar to bamboo but smaller in diameter. The plaited strips often meshed so a sharp end was left protruding above the floor rather than secured beneath it. Sometimes a sharpened end once properly concealed would pop out as the result of a heavy footstep on a different area of the floor. Such booby traps were common, and visitors to my house would occasionally grimace in pain as a naked toe kicked one of the sharp points. I offered this hypothesis. A check of each foot in the room laid it limply to rest.

This was female menstrual blood, the worst kind. Male anger built as it was pointed out that Wareia would no doubt become ill. He might even die, although it was unlikely. But the blood had posed the same threat to each man present. After all, any one of them might have taken his seat where the unfortunate Wareia had plunked down. The initial panic gradually gave way to seeming calm. With any luck the furor would blow over and I could get back to the business of collecting data. In a totally unanticipated way, that is exactly what happened.

Turi's wife Nabene came running from next door. The fleeing boys had spread the bare outline of the calamitous situation. As she entered, Nabene was instructed to clean up the offending spot of blood. She sent one of her small brothers-in-law for a rag. While awaiting his return she fought a constant battle to stifle her giggling. Each time she looked at Wareia she burst into a huge smile. She hid her face, turned away, and generally fought the impulse to burst into laughter at his discomfort, which she later suggested seemed a bit histrionic. Nabene was herself a notorious tease. On one occasion of my morning meeting, she had been seated at my hearth when Yombi entered and sat down. The first man to enter, he assumed the role of inspecting the floor for the toxic pollutants women too often leave in their wake. He pointed to a piece of grass that had become dislodged from a woman's skirt. He ordered Nabene to pick it up and put it on the fire. Destroying it would avoid the sort of calamity I was now observing. Yombi turned his attention away from the direction of Nabene toward me. Nabene, sitting directly opposite me and fully in my view, picked up the piece of dried and yellowed grass. She held it out before her, smiled impishly at me, and placed it gently across Yombi's leg. His hard, dry skin failed to inform him immediately of the violation. Nabene sat quietly, listening to our discussion. I decided to pretend that I had not witnessed Nabene's action. Finally, as if assaulted by an insignificant but noticeable itch, Yombi reached out to scratch his knee. Touching the piece of grass, he glanced to inspect what his hand had encountered. He gasped, and flicked the grass from his leg much as he might have done to a disgusting creature. Nabene lapsed into convulsive laughter. Yombi glanced at his daughter-in-law in shocked disbelief. He threatened her with his machete and sent her (still laughing) from the house. He turned to me, the trace of a smile on his face. Shaking his head, he described Nabene as *longlong* (crazy).

When Nabene had completed her assignment and the spot had been removed, the men resumed their seats around my hearth. Discussion now shifted to the determination of the guilty party. Which women had been in my house over the past few days? I chose to maintain my silence as one name after another was offered up. By the end of this phase of the discussion, it was obvious to me that all movements to and from my house were public knowledge. I had always known this to be the case, but such open discussion of those movements highlighted the general absence of privacy in village affairs. I also learned, although I chose not to record the information in my field notes, the menstrual cycle of nearly every one of my close female informants and most of my casual female visitors.

That this entire episode was little more than an Imbonggu enactment of a kangaroo court soon became apparent. It was unanimously decided that the guilty party was none other than Peni. Like a courtroom observer, I listened from beyond the central stage upon which the characters played out their roles. I was present, but my presence was not required. The drama took a decidedly conspiratorial turn. Men leaned close to one another, whispered in muffled tones, nodded heads. Turi was awarded the role of court bailiff. He dutifully, and hesitantly, informed me that Peni had committed a very bad act. She had polluted my house, possibly injured Wareia, and threatened the health of each man present at the event. Some men watched me intently. Others averted their gazes in different directions. The damaged section of my floor would be torn out and replaced. I would pay two men two kina each when they completed the task. And from this day, no women would enter my house except with Yombi's approval.

Fortunately, I was too dumbstruck to respond immediately. Back in Pittsburgh I would have no doubt blurted out "You must be out of your minds!" or something equally clever. The fact I had no ready response provided me the opportunity to actually think rather than merely react with hostility. I agreed that this entire affair was truly unfortunate, but I was certain Wareia would not die. I would, of course, compensate him adequately. Heads nodded approvingly at my acknowledgment of responsibility. Still, there was the issue of the women. Firmly, I stated that though Yombi had built my house, the fact remained that I had paid him for doing so. I continued to compensate him for his labor by paying the annual head tax for him, his son Turi, and their wives. The house was mine, and only I would decide who enjoyed the privilege of entering it. Further, I would decide who would not enter as well.

Men squirmed. Turi's lower lip crept up and engulfed its upper twin, signaling the degree of his perplexed reaction to my rejection of the men's verdict and sentence. No, he was certain that Yombi would bar entry to women when he heard of the incident. I lowered my eyes, frantically evaluating what I took to be my options. After a few seconds, I stared Turi in the eye and declared that I would not wait for Yombi to offer an edict that was not his to offer. I would leave the village that morning. I could not live in a house where others set such restrictions on me and my guests. I was truly saddened, because moving to another village would be a terrible waste of my limited time among the Imbonggu. It would also mean that I would have to pay a great deal of my money to the men of a different village to build a new house for me. Sadly, there seemed no other option. I scanned the eyes boring into me in search of some reaction to my bluff. There was only incomprehension. I slowly realized that I was actually thinking what each of the men was fearing: I was not bluffing!

I set about packing my small notebooks into my canvas military shoulder bag and indicated my plan to walk to the government station. Once there, I would secure a truck to transport my gear from the village before the afternoon rains arrived. Taking my cue, men got to their feet and drifted out of the house. A cluster of children formed a rear-guard observer team outside my house as if to report whether or not I actually made further preparations to leave. Inside the house I was becoming increasingly furious at the whole absurd situation. At the same time, I became steadily more comfortable with my decision to leave if the men did not back down from their stance.

About fifteen minutes later, the men returned. They followed a somber Yombi into my house. He took a seat at my hearth. The others followed suit. As a prelude to what he obviously feared would be a difficult session, Yombi fumbled through the pockets of his once new, but now ratty and never washed, jacket. His exploration failed to turn up any tobacco. I handed him a pack of cigarettes. He took one, and extended the pack weakly in my direction with the unspoken "Do you really want the rest of these?" I motioned the pack back with a casual wave of my hand. He passed the pack around. It disappeared. Was it true that I had told these men I was moving to another village? All this inconvenience over a woman. And a lazy one, no less. He tried to explain that the decision to ban women from the house was best for all concerned. Feeling antagonistic, I reminded him that a few dozen women were involved and the ban did not seem best for them. Yombi's silence suggested he was unimpressed with the argument.

Yombi took another tack. The ban was really in my own best interests. After all, if the women were not banned from the house, the men might refuse to visit. How would I learn all the things the men might tell me if they did not come to my house as a result of concern for their safety? I would take that risk, I responded. At least a person's absence from my hearth would be his own decision. After much verbal maneuvering we blundered into a possible compromise. Women would be permitted to enter my house, but they must sit on only one side of the hearth. That way their polluting influence would be localized. Since men would under no circumstance sit on the women's side of the hearth, they could avoid the horrendous risks posed by the women. The remaining three sides of the hearth would be reserved for the men. This treaty was seldom violated.

The compromise so far described was decidedly a victory for the anthropologist and a monument to the utility of coercive power in interpersonal relations. If I left the village, all my valuables would go with me. No more cigarettes, kerosene, rice, disinfectant and bandages, shortwave radio, and so forth. Most important, no more ready cash for loans or payment of trumped-up compensation claims. I negotiated from the more powerful position. In their effort to salvage some small measure of success, the final component of the compromise guaranteed that I, like all the men concerned, would suffer some loss of face. Peni would be banned permanently from the house. Yombi assured me with grim resignation that this condition was not negotiable. I thought for a few seconds. I reasoned that given the way things normally occurred, it was highly likely that the whole issue would be forgotten soon enough and that Peni could quietly reclaim her most-favored-visitor status. Conceding (actually a case of *grisim*) that Yombi was tough but fair, I agreed to his compromise.

I often chuckled to myself when my house was packed to the rafters with women and young girls, all bunched atop one another on one side of the hearth, while two or three men shared the remaining three-quarters of my front room. This bizarre seating arrangement offered a constant reminder of the incident. Sadly, what might be referred to as the Peni Compromise also held. She continued to visit, both by herself and in the company of other women, but never again did truly enter my house. She normally sat in the doorway or just outside the door. The doorway became the frame for the stage on which she was forbidden to set foot. Sensing that she was more observer than participant, she often drifted away unnoticed. On other occasions, normally when she came alone or if it were raining, she would stretch the interpretation of the Peni Compromise to mean that if she were not fully inside the house then she was not in the house at all. She would gradually ease her way inside until only a leg or a foot remained extended through the doorway, visible to the ever vigilant eyes of interested passersby. It occurred to me on one such occasion that there was a great deal of similarity between my house in Tona and my freshman college dormitory, with its female-visitor rules demanding that the door remain open and that host and guest each keep at least one foot on the floor at all times.

12 / Women on the Outside

The Imbi occupy the southwesternmost pocket of Imbonggu territory. Their tip of the triangle converges with similar territories belonging to the Wiru and Kewa, whose languages are different from one another and Imbonggu. Other pockets of Imbonggu share boundaries with speakers of different languages including Mendi and Enga. Women from all these groups are married to Imbonggu men and live in Nagop and Tona. It is accepted that men are free to marry as many wives as they can obtain and care for. In fact, there are few such polygynous men. The majority of marriages are monogamous, involving a single man and a lone wife. Whether a man is a polygynist depends largely on his access to wealth and his political ambitions. Men with more than one wife do not necessarily marry women from a single neighboring language group. Thus, a single family might include an Imbonggu man, his Mendi, Wiru, and Kewa wives, and the children of all three wives. The children might speak all four languages with varying degrees of fluency. They might also speak English if they have attended either the Catholic or government primary school. In addition, they might speak Neo-Melanesian, particularly if a brother works for the government or has spent some time away from the village working at a distant plantation or town. Tiny linguists abound in an Imbonggu village, unlike the average town in America.

Such foreign women who marry Imbonggu men seldom become totally fluent in Imbonggu. Husbands seldom spend a great deal of time talking with wives in casual conversation. Men speak to men, quite secure in the knowledge that women are unlikely to add anything significant to the usual topics of conversation. Imbonggu men not only see their wives as linguistically illiterate, but also as somewhat lacking intellectually. I frequently observed men playing card games for the purpose of gambling. Women might observe, if they did so quietly, outside the circle of men. By contrast, when women played the same games, men hovered over them offering constant advice, criticism, and abuse. Men often explained, "Women cannot think like men."

By contrast, interaction among women is intense and personal. Women tend to cluster around one another on the basis of shared language and home village. Thus women continue to speak Wiru or Kewa while in the gardens or at market. Daughters and young sons accompany mothers to the gardens daily and may sleep separate from their fathers in the house of the mother. They learn the languages of their mothers as a result. The children of polygynous men may include half-siblings whose mothers speak different languages. As a result, they may learn to speak the languages of each of their father's wives. But the women themselves seldom learn to speak languages other than their own. In linguistic terms, an Imbonggu village is

An Imbi village typically surrounds a central ceremonial ground that is in turn encircled by gardens of sweet potato and sugar cane.

comprised of a male Imbonggu-speaking core surrounded by satellite clusters of women who speak different languages. Daughters will stay on the outside, with their mothers. Sons, as they mature, will gravitate to the core. This linguistic pattern is loosely reproduced in the spatial arrangement of the village. Around a central dance ground are the houses of the men of the core. The houses of the wives are built outside that circle. They often sit among the gardens the women tend, or in the tall grass along the paths radiating outward from the central cluster of men's houses toward the gardens, the bush, or other villages. Seldom are the houses of wives within view of the houses of their husbands.

The social worlds of men and women differ in more than merely language and spatial arrangement. Anthropologists have written volumes on the subject of the division of labor in society. Two of the more prominent factors underlying that division are age and sex. For the Imbonggu, age is a generally insignificant factor. Children lack the strength and experience of their parents and older siblings, but they perform the same tasks. They are merely less efficient. Elderly men and women experience loss of speed, dexterity, and strength, as well as suffer all the other infirmities of age, but they continue to perform the same tasks as their adult children. Like their grandchildren, they are simply less efficient in terms of output.

Sex is the major factor in the Imbonggu division of labor. Men see themselves as hunters, although the virtual absence of game brought to the hearth suggests that they are either nearly totally lacking in hunting skills or were at one time phenomenally successful, to the point at which all the game in their territory was exhausted by their efforts. The latter explanation seems far less likely. Men keep dogs for the stated purpose of tracking and cornering game. In my experience these untrained dogs were useless in the hunt. In sum, men as hunters provide no measurable contribution to Imbi diet.

Women are responsible for the bulk of horticultural tasks. Once men have cleared a garden area, women begin the work of agriculture. Men often describe the clearing as "heavy" work women cannot do. Women agree. Anthropologists are often faced with the fact of behavior that is at odds with the stated reasons for its performance. To what degree is the anthropologist bound to credit the explanations of informants rather than the testimony of his or her own observations and impressions? It is not so simple a question. The Imbi clearing of sweet potato gardens is such an instance. Sweet potato gardens are invariably located near the village on substantially level ground with a cover of grass as opposed to forest. Clearing such areas involves no more than the repeated swinging of a bush knife, an activity far less demanding than many (if not most) performed by women. In fact, in the cases of truly lazy husbands, I observed women performing the clearing of grasses to make way for gardens. Despite male claims that male strength was required to do such clearing, and female agreement, I have reason to suspect that women agree as a form of blatant flattery designed to encourage men to contribute at least some labor to the process. But no informant, male or female, ever openly admitted the correctness of my conclusion. Men could not bring themselves to admit that women were capable of doing something ostensibly demanding male strength. Women would understandably admit to nothing that would result in the loss of a husband's labor contribution, no matter how slight it might be.

In any event, once the land is cleared, women embark on the business of producing the bulk of the Imbi food supply in the form of several varieties of sweet potato. The cut grass is collected into piles for later use. The soil must be broken to facilitate planting. Two primary means are employed. Long poles may be jabbed into the earth to break it up. The resulting large lumps of earth are then further fractured by blows with a bush knife. A second strategy is to tether pigs in the new garden area for a few days. Their rooting around effectively breaks up the soil with a great reduction in the amount of female labor required. Once the ground is broken, a woman defines a circle approximately six feet in diameter. In the middle she piles some of the cut grass, which will act as a mulching agent. She then moves around the circle throwing soil from the outside into the center. She performs this routine repeatedly until the garden area is full of such small dome-shaped mounds. Each mound is usually elevated at the center to a point approximately two feet above the level of its circumference at the base.

Women perform the business of constructing garden mounds either in pairs or larger teams whose labor contribution is reciprocated at a later time. Mound-building is often a time of social release for women. They exploit the opportunity to discuss any pressing problems that do not receive a sympathetic listening among their Imbonggu husbands. Such a group of women working in company also provides an opportunity for gossip and playful joking. By themselves, away from the demands and orders of their husbands, women enjoy the opportunity simply to have a good laugh at the expense of husbands and fathers-in-law.

When the mound is completely shaped, living sweet potato vines are inserted

Nabene working in her garden constructing sweet potato mounds

around the surface. Women will do some slight weeding over the next few months, but from this point on women largely wait for the tubers to mature inside the mound. About six months later the harvesting of the mound begins. Since people and pigs require sweet potato on a daily basis, women perform their mounding labors in a cyclical pattern so as to guarantee that some portion of their total garden land is always in the harvesting phase.

The food requirements for which a woman is responsible may be considerable. She must provide adequate food for her husband, her adolescent sons, the pigs in her care, herself, and her daughters, more or less in that order of significance. Pigs contribute up to a point. They may be tethered in an abandoned garden area during the day, allowing them to root around for what small tubers remain once further harvesting is no longer efficient in terms of yield relative to labor input. Women agree that this reduces the amount of sweet potato they must carry back to the house in the evening to feed to their pigs. It often seems a questionable strategy, as the casual observer might be forgiven for concluding that Imbonggu pigs specialize in two primary activities: eating and what physicists might term the "equal and opposite" action. Imbi women recognize the same truth. They take advantage of the situation by planting vegetable gardens atop the fertile remains of pig houses abandoned after years of use.

In addition to her pigs, the woman must daily provide food for her husband, herself, and her children. She may return from the garden directly to her house and begin to roast or boil the evening meal of sweet potato, usually with rice and various vegetables. Or she may stop initially at her husband's house and leave sweet potato for him and her sons to roast at their own fire. She and her daughters normally eat in her house. The demands of pigs and husbands are more or less absolute and are seldom subject to negotiation. If she has failed to bring enough sweet potato from the garden, she and her daughters will suffer the shortage. It is not uncommon to see young girls rising early in the morning to forage for their own food if no sweet potato is left for their morning meal. Girls collect large grasshoppers clinging to trees, still immobilized by the morning cold and dew. These roasted morsels provide an occasional substitute for sweet potato.

The relationship of women and pigs is more than one of steward on the one hand and occasional provider of garden labor on the other. Women, children, and pigs often share houses. Women look after piglets as they do their children. Piglets are given names and tended to when ill. A small pig, like a small child, may be carried in a *bilum* bag suspended over a woman's back and held in place by a huge knot resting against her forehead. In a very real sense, women and pigs are locked in a reproductive relationship of primary benefit to men. As a result of a woman's care and effort, a man's pig herd will be enlarged over the years. As his pig herd enlarges, a man enjoys a greater opportunity to obtain additional wives. This endless positive feedback loop forever links women and pigs among the Imbonggu. A wife provides a very real form of reproductive labor by caring for a pig herd that men actively seek to enlarge at the expense of female labor in maintenance of this wealth on the hoof. There seems little mystery concerning this aspect of the sexual antagonism that characterizes highlands New Guinea societies such as the Imbonggu.

The issue of the place and role of the sexes in exchange systems such as that of the Imbonggu has been hotly debated among anthropologists. It is related to the

Imbi women tend pigs much as they do their human families.

earlier discussion of brideprice versus bridewealth and the role of women in the arranging of marriages. To what extent do women participate actively in such transactions and negotiations as opposed to merely being passive pawns? In recent years, one effect of the feminist perspective has been the emergence of a body of literature documenting more active female participation in highlands New Guinea exchange systems (Josephides 1985; Lederman 1986; M. Strathern 1972). There has certainly been much more thorough investigation of the activities of women in the sphere of economic exchange with the emergence of a feminist perspective in anthropology. Unlike the brideprice debate that has been essentially revisionist in nature, the contemporary research into female economic activity has coincided with an unprecedented expansion of female participation, rather than a mere attempt to rewrite anthropological history. Mendi women are reported to own ceremonial valuables and to exchange such items on public occasions (Lederman 1986:117–140). Imbonggu women do not presently enjoy such prominence in public affairs.

At the same time there is some reason to predict that Imbonggu women may come to enjoy increasing freedom in economic areas. In the 1970s a dramatic turnaround (at least among the Imbi) occurred in the area of elementary school enrollments. Sons had long been the favored candidates to benefit from public education. Fathers hoped that their sons would learn enough to gain government employment and the advantages in salary and housing that came with it. After they adhered to this strategy for years, the desired results never materialized. Frustrated by the fact that sons were not obtaining wage employment, fathers decided that to pay additional school fees for the next group of sons was to throw good money after bad. They adopted a new strategy. They consciously opted to send their daughters to school. Their reasoning was that their daughters might become educated to the point where they could attract an employed worker as a husband! Not exactly a liberating movement, but an opportunity for girls nonetheless. This notion that girls could not learn the skills that would lead to employment was consistent with the Imbonggu view that women are inherently less capable than men. At the same time there seems little doubt that the emergence of a generation of relatively better educated Imbonggu women will considerably improve the status of women generally, as well as their economic prospects.

Imbonggu women happen to be at the beginning of their trek to increased independence. Their Mendi and Melpa neighbors started earlier and have experienced greater progress. At the other end of the highlands region is the Eastern Highlands. Women there, particularly in the Daulo region, provide the current model for highlands women and possibly a prediction of things to come for the women of less-developed regions of the highlands. The women of the Daulo have initiated active participation in the cash economy and have organized *Wok Meri* cooperatives that manage the money earned by women through the sale of coffee and other economic ventures (Sexton 1986). While this may be reason for optimism, Imbonggu women continue to operate on the fringe, their activities largely in the service of the men who dominate from the core.

13 / "The White Man Will Eat You!"

Children are everywhere in Imbonggu. Over half the population was twelve years of age or younger when I first arrived in Tona. Almost all were extremely curious about me. I was the first white person many had ever seen. I was the only white person who had ever lived in a house in the village. On very rare occasions government and mission personnel entered the village, carried out a specific task, and returned to their enclave at the end of the project, or when the afternoon rains started, whichever occurred first. I was not only a novelty to be observed, but a mystery to be explained.

I was also a fact of daily life in the village, intent on prying into everyone's business. But I also shared my hearth, house, food, radio, torch, and other possessions with the Imbi. I had acquired a kinship niche by virtue of Yombi having given me access to some land and providing me with sugar cane plants. Nabene had given me sweet potato vines to establish my garden. And Yombi and Turi had built my house. Extended kinship ties were somewhat defined by these generally accepted nuclear ties, but not entirely. Some Imbi were uncertain whether I was best defined as a distant relative against whom some more limited claims could be made for food, money, and so forth. Others felt that I was best regarded as an outsider until I had proven my sincerity. For many of those, relationships emerged over time. For others, I was an outsider until the day I left, in much the same way that some of my upstate New York schoolmates were still "City kids" even after living for years in the town where I grew up.

Definitions of my social position were varied and fascinating. One of my dearest friends was an aging man whose house was located only a few meters from mine, but socially outside the village's inner circle. While I found him warm and sensitive, most Imbi held him in relatively low esteem. His kin relationship ties to me, had he chosen to accept common form, would have been weak and unrewarding. He confided in me early that he was concerned for me. After all, my wife was in Australia. While women are dangerous and troublesome in a variety of ways, it nonetheless remains a fact that no man should be without one. Therefore, I could marry his daughter. We could agree to a minimal brideprice payment, he would become my father-in-law, and he would protect me against some people who he feared were intent on exploiting me. My reluctance to take advantage of his proposition was the source of considerable concern to him throughout my years of residence with the Imbi.

But there is more to Imbi life than simply being related in some way to all one's fellow Imbi. Imbi are a society, and one in which everyone pulls his or her weight. That means contributing to the social health of the community. So Torol knew how

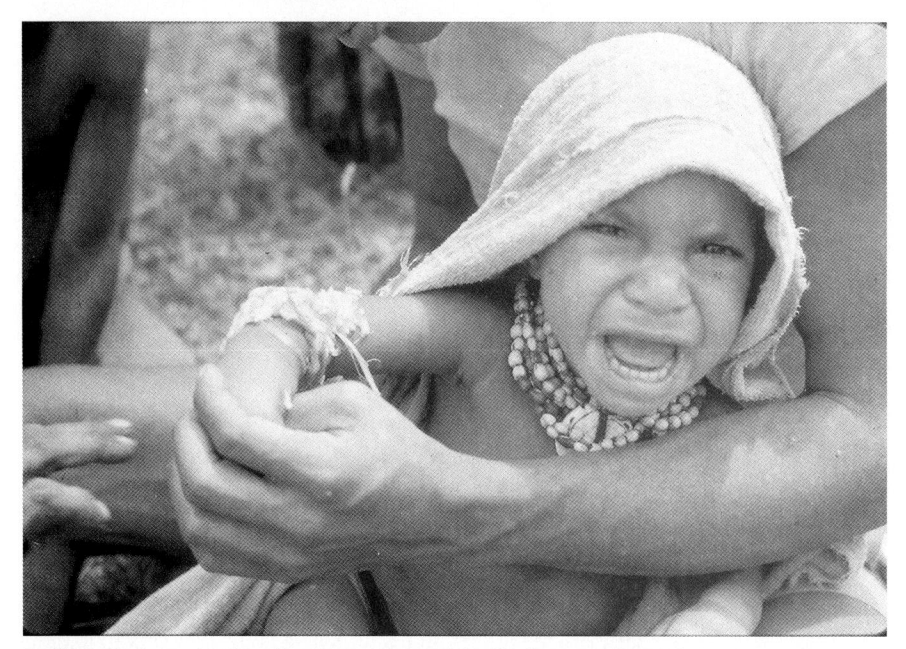

Indipendo in pain; her burn was dressed by Kelo, an acknowledged expert on such treatments.

to make sorcery. Kelo knew the art of muscle manipulation. Yama knew the stories of the sacred stones. Wakea knew the art of love magic. Everyone had a role. What could mine be? It is not an easy thing to place a physically mature adult in a responsible adult role when he or she exhibits the social and cultural knowledge of a two-year-old who constantly says no when he means yes and vice versa.

As time passed, however, many roles emerged for me. One the Imbi valued highly was that of tourist attraction. Visitors literally walked miles to observe the white man who chose to live in an Imbi village house. Such visitors brought with them gifts of food and welcome news of relatives living in other villages. They shared their stories and opinions and inquired into mine. I found that I was a better anthropologist than informant. This demanded attention, as the Imbi were not about to spend their evenings telling me their stories without some form of reciprocation. But my repertoire of myths and legends proved to be nearly nonexistent. Paul Bunyan and his ox held possibilities, but my incomplete familiarity with it left the Imbi unsatisfied. That a giant ox could leave depressions and lakes in his wake made considerable sense to the Imbi, whose every stride accomplished the same feat. But there was no moral to be learned, or at least none to be learned from me.

I needed something more. George Washington came to mind. He held at least the prospect of moral instruction. But I came to accept the Imbi view that throwing a coin across a river is a somewhat strange thing to do. As a feat of prowess, it left the Imbi unimpressed. Not surprising, really. After all, the widest river in the experience of most is about twelve feet. Truly adventurous men who had gone to the Nebilyer to return with wives could visualize a river as wide as fifty feet. Pawa pointed out that even his sixteen-year-old daughter could throw a stone across the Nebilyer. Being able to recall only the bare bones of the story, I was unable to explain what facts had possessed a grown man to throw a coin across a river. But the mere fact he would throw money away like that was a clear symptom of dementia in the Imbi interpretation.

But I was not yet willing to consign America's first president to the unimportant and insignificant. There remained the famous cherry tree. At last, proclaimed Pawa, we were getting somewhere. All men should carry an axe and know how to cut trees. There was hope after all for this enigmatic white hero. That he had learned to use an axe in his youth was what every Imbi father would expect. It was unsurprising that he would cut a tree whose value was greater than he thought. All Imbi boys sooner or later make the same mistake. The story was progressing well, approving heads nodding from every corner of my house. Finally we reached the moral conclusion. To the disbelief of the Imbi, George had admitted to cutting the tree that was not his to cut. The nodding stopped, and the eyes that had earlier focused on me were now turned to one another and back to me. The silence suggested that I had no more to say. It also hinted that no Imbi knew what to say or how to say it.

My mind raced through all the Imbi stories I had heard, in a frantic effort to relate my tale of the value of truth to one the Imbi could appreciate. Awareness hit me like a blow to the stomach. I had not yet heard any Imbi story suggesting that telling the truth was a worthwhile endeavor. During the remainder of my time with the Imbi no such story was destined to echo around my hearth. The Imbi refuse to accept that lying is intrinsically wrong. They are in good company. Plato questioned the notion also. One of the endearing qualities of enemies, of which the Imbi like all New Guinea Highlanders have an endless supply, is that they are indeed supposed to lie. Even when they are telling the truth, one must assume one's enemies are lying. No matter what the Ango say, one must always be skeptical of their veracity. But this skepticism, bordering on cynicism, also places the Imbi in good company. After all, one of the primary responsibilities of the U.S. Department of State is to interpret for the American people what the world's Communists truly mean when they issue a communiqué. Exactly as the Imbi, most Americans grow up learning that our enemies are compulsive liars. If a point was to be taken away from the story of George Washington and the cherry tree, I concluded, surely it must be that American children are retarded in their social development by accepting the wisdom of such stories for even a short time before the true facts of social interaction are learned. Clearly, my inability to tell stories worth listening to caused me much concern, although my house continued to be a destination for distant friends and relatives of the Imbi. The situation took a turn for the better when I happened across a copy of Kipling's *Just So Stories*. They were very well received.

A second role of mine was that of status symbol. Many white persons lived in the Ialibu area, most commonly as government contract workers, missionaries, teachers, or foreign volunteers. But I was the only one who lived in an Imbonggu village. There was always much interest in my comings and goings. My Imbi clan mates took delight in introducing me as their *kondodl* (red man). The Imbonggu are not color blind. Far from it. They describe what they see. I am often amazed at a system of ethnic classification that demands that I and several million of my coloring tick off "white" simply because it is what we have been told we are. The Imbi and their Papua New Guinean comrades find no difficulty achieving more accurate descriptions. Wendy Patrick, a friend from Milne Bay Province, always referred to white people by the Neo-Melanesian term *dimdim*. It was never totally clear to me whether she was describing their skin or their wits. But whether white, red, or dim, one thing remained clear: I stuck out in Imbonggu crowds.

In an effort to confirm their privileged claim to me and my resources, Imbi always linked my kinship position to their proprietary interest in me. The message was clear: I was not fair game. I, and my wealth, belonged to the Imbi. My presence was also taken to mean that the Imbi enjoyed closer access to the government's resources through me. While there was no truth to this rumor, it refused to go away.

To my distress, I was also defined as something of a medical practitioner. I had spoken with numerous anthropologists and read in many books about the common phenomenon of anthropologist-as-doctor. This role concerned me a great deal. When I was discharged from the U.S. Army at Fort Lewis, Washington, in 1968, I humiliated myself by passing out as I watched an enormous quantity of my blood being sucked into a hypodermic needle the size of a baseball bat. There would be no point in taking such needles to the field with me. Beyond the personal wimp factor was the realization that I had no idea what was contained in most medicines. I had always consumed the potions prescribed by my own doctors, but I had granted them my confidence in their knowledge and training. Possessing neither, I refused to yield to the temptation to enter the field with enormous quantities of drugs and syringes. My response to all injuries was basic. I cleansed the wound with Dettol, an over-the-counter disinfectant, applied enough gauze to cover the wound, and referred the victim of the calamity to the health center about five miles away. This satisfied my concerns about a weak stomach, medical ignorance, and the moral issue of usurping the medical profession's widely accepted role of playing God. Still, I cleaned enough axe wounds, machete wounds, knife wounds, and burns to qualify as a medical doctor through a fully accredited, credit-for-life program. But one appeal of my medicine chest to the Imbi was exactly what defined its limitations to me: its mystery. All Imbi cures are in the hands of specialists in their application. That is not to say that one person knows and applies them all. Quite the contrary, few practitioners understand more than one or two cures, of which there are dozens. Under these circumstances nothing is unique about possessing or dispensing medicine. The Imbi never quite understood my reluctance to dispense my potions. Uncertainty of success was inadequate justification. After all, the Imbi had the same problem. Nothing works all the time. My ignorance of how cures worked was equally unacceptable as a justification for my apparent selfishness. No Imbi practitioner possessed such knowledge. All cures were learned from *tumbuna*. Ancestors passed on the application of medical technology rather than medical knowledge itself. "We have always done it that way" is surely the most frustrating response an anthropologist can receive. We want knowledge, not just habit. Yala, on my refusal to give him aspirin, pointed out that he didn't care how it worked. He merely wanted his headache to go away. Once again the table had been turned on me. After all, Americans gulp aspirin for the primary purpose of alleviating pain. Despite the frivolity of television commercials depicting little colored spheres bouncing around inside our bodies on some mysteriously predetermined timed-release schedule, most Americans have absolutely no knowledge of how aspirin works in the body and what it accomplishes aside from the desired alleviation of pain!

My most intriguing role, if the least personally rewarding, was that of legendary, semimythological creature. It turned out that my mere glance, or even a distant reference to me, was sufficient to frighten children into doing what all their developing urges convinced them they did not want to do. When I announced my intention to live in a village in the highlands of New Guinea, friends and relatives were normally dumbstruck. "Wasn't that where Michael Rockefeller was eaten by cannibals?" was a common response. Or, "Don't they still eat people there?" No amount of reassurance on my part could serve to allay those fears. Looking back, I am certain that the news of my trip to New Guinea was as troublesome to my parents as my military orders sending me to Vietnam a few years earlier. The Social Security Administration need not fear making payments to Bill Wormsley if he persisted in his reckless lifestyle.

But as my stay with the Imbi lengthened, they assured me that my concerned family and friends had been correct. There were cannibals and sorcerers, the Imbi assured me. But fortunately for me, I was not living among them. Had I opted for any other village in the basin, however, that would not be the case. But there was a problem. Every Ialibu clan and village where I discussed the matter told me exactly the same thing. It seemed that only the names were changed to identify the innocent, the cannibals, and the sorcerers. Old women in the village cried when I made a trip to Mount Hagen. The Hagen people were almost certain to kill me. A trip to Wabag all but triggered my mourning rites. The Enga were an absolute certainty to kill me, even if they chose not to eat me. And, of course, a trip to the coastal town of Lae was the most inexplicable form of flirting with disaster. I would have to travel through the lands of the Chimbu. These unfathomable people were known to laugh at the death of a person and cry at the purchase of a new truck. Such demented behavior defied rational explanation. Such people could only be dangerous in the extreme. On my only return trip from Lae, one of the old women of the village froze at the sight of me. As recognition set in, she screamed, dropped her woven net bag of sweet potatoes and baby piglet, and ran toward her house yelling to all who could hear that a ghost was in the village. I could only speculate at the wild tales about my trip that must have been told in my absence.

Anthropologist William Arens (1979) has written a fascinating history and analysis of the study of cannibalism and its attribution to groups of people throughout recorded history. The book proved to be quite controversial, for no apparent reason. Reading his book in light of my experiences among the Imbonggu, I thought his argument so basic and so obvious as to militate against the sort of debate that ensued. There are no cannibals, or at least not in the numbers reported or for the purposes reported. To say that someone else is a cannibal is to define him as less than human. Accepting the unavoidability of occasionally having to kill others in order to defend or promote one's own interests requires that some strategy be employed to redefine the basic fact of humanness on both sides of a dispute or war. So Americans were told by their government that Japanese committed every conceivable atrocity during the Second World War. The Japanese told their citizens and soldiers the same things about Americans. As historian John Dower (1986) illustrates, no one should be surprised at the realization that most atrocities committed by the combatants against one another during the Second World War occurred in the Pacific theater, between American and Japanese soldiers. German and Italian soldiers were never dehumanized to the same extent by the Allies. Likewise, the European Axis powers treated the Allies comparably. The major atrocities of the European war were committed against Jewish noncombatants. Japanese and American reciprocal charges of atrocities and cannibalism thus provided just one more form of legitimization for the need to kill one another. The cannibals of the Ialibu Basin perform that same essential role in sociopolitical conflict.

But other cannibals are afoot among the Imbi. They are horrible creatures. Some possess no mouths. The tops of their heads are hinged at the back and can be lifted up. In this manner food is consumed through the top of the heads of these mouthless monsters. In all other physical respects they closely resemble human beings. Because of their anatomy, they are limited in their consumption to smaller humans, especially children. The threat of being set outside at night to be collected and dropped into the open skull of this monster is a powerful force in Imbi behavior modification techniques. Children seldom persist in the behavior that leads an angry mother to threaten to offer her child as a spirit-meal. Such monsters are not a stock cast of supernatural characters. Imbonggu storytellers are wonderfully talented in the arts of invention and embellishment. New monsters are created as needed or desired. But the utility of all these monsters, mouthless or otherwise, is mitigated somewhat by one unfortunate fact. No one has ever seen one. And, of course, maturing children come to question their existence. Indipendo, a young girl of six or seven years of age, was displaying an unusual tendency to question authority. And just as American and European children come to forfeit belief in the bogeymen that keep them out of the cellar, Indipendo was on the verge of concluding that no mouthless, hinged-headed monsters existed in the real world.

One evening as several people sat around my hearth, Indipendo pressed her mother, Alu, beyond the limit of her patience. Indipendo was unmoved by reference to the mouthless monster. In a fit of inspiration, Alu recalled Indipendo's discomfort at the noise of airplanes, which the young girl had never seen up close but feared considerably. Indipendo often asked about the *balus* spirit when she heard planes pass overhead. In one final attempt at maintaining control of her headstrong daughter, Alu explained that *balus* was something white men knew about. It opened a giant hole in its side through which people entered the monster. People went in the monster's gut, but only spirits came out. Indipendo, skeptical of the description but still leery of the machines themselves, expressed her cautious disbelief. Alu proceeded to note that *balus* took people to the land of white men, where they were eaten. Only white men returned. The few Imbonggu who returned had become like white men, but most never returned. In the mind of a child, never is a somewhat imprecise concept. But young men often left the village to work on plantations or to seek their fortunes in the big city of Port Moresby. Such young men were often absent for years at a stretch. Village children knew of such youths but almost never saw them return. When the youths did make the trek back to Tona, they wore the

Nabene smiles and Nasil cries, a typical greeting for anthropologists with cannibalistic tendencies.

Nervous Kanambo attempts to crawl into the woodwork to avoid the stare of the anthropologist.

white man's clothing and carried his tape cassette players and wristwatches, the latter always a mystery to the Imbi.

Alu's desperate attempt was beginning to take shape in a most unlikely way. Intent on pressing her emerging advantage, she continued. She noted that I had come to Ialibu inside *balus*. Several onlookers assented. Indipendo appraised me and shifted perceptibly closer to her mother. All the village children had heard stories of how white men "thumped" New Guineans, put them into jail, and killed them by hanging them from trees. Younger Imbi children had always given me a wide berth, but we were now on the verge of being consigned to different universes. Seeking balance, Alu assured Indipendo that I had promised not to eat anyone while I lived in Tona. But like Alu, I might be pushed beyond my tolerance, and this could not be good. Then Alu drove the final nail into my coffin when she threatened, "If you misbehave, I will give you to Kondoli, and he will eat you!"

For the remainder of my stay, young children of Tona often would run screaming in search of their mothers at my approach. As they matured, even the threat of Kondoli eating them lost its potency. But while the threat evaporated for individual children, it continued to be offered to the younger ones as they tended toward disobedience. It became a common occurrence for a song or story to be interrupted with a stern, "Be quiet. Or the White Man will eat you!"

14 / Rich Men Give It All Away

Anthropologists have described an impressive array of political leadership models. The truly egalitarian model focuses on the simple headman. Merely one among equals, the headman enjoys neither structural nor hereditary claim to power. In fact, he holds no power at all in the coercive sense. His legitimacy comes from the willingness of his followers to accept his decisions and advice. By contrast, chiefdoms are led by men who boast a hereditary claim to their position. Their power is often absolute and structural in nature. Commoners do not question the decisions or decrees of chiefs.

The Imbonggu have neither headmen nor chiefs. Like other Melanesians, the Imbonggu have a political structure based on a particular model described as the Big Man (Sahlins 1963). Yombi, who built my house, who sought to control access to it, who placed me in his kinship circle, who provided cuttings for my garden, is a Big Man. It was that status that permitted him to establish his claim to me despite the wishes of several other men to stake a similar claim. Sadly, Yombi had no daughter within a decade of marriageable age. Thus, he could not make first claim to incorporate me into his family as a son-in-law, as so many others sought to do.

Yombi's rise to political prominence would be difficult for most Americans to understand. He was not elected. As a Big Man, Yombi had no reason to concern himself with votes. Neither did his prominence flow from some preordained position in a hereditary line of succession to power. No royal blood courses through Yombi's veins. In a sense, like all Big Men, Yombi is every bit the self-made man. He established himself as a dependable broker. The commodities he maneuvered and manipulated were wealth, knowledge, and the expectations of others. The markets or arenas within which he demonstrated his strengths and amassed his followers included the production of massive ceremonial exchanges of valued items of wealth (pigs and pearl shells), the negotiation and accumulation of brideprice, and the public resolution of disputes. He was justly proud of his impressive accomplishments in these areas and took advantage of most any opportunity to remind listeners of those successes. But one evening he confided to me that there was another ingredient in the formula, one over which he had far less control. American basketball great Bill Russell once said, "I'd rather be lucky than good." After all, one can be very good, possibly even great, and lose nevertheless. But, reasoned Russell, "lucky" implies a positive outcome, ignoring for the moment the equally enticing wisdom of those immortal country and western music lyrics, "If I had no bad luck, I'd have no luck at all!" Apparently preferring basketball to Nashville, Yombi admitted that there was no human-made substitute for the fortuitous message of a singing bird or the prescient dream of a dreamer. Inevitably

Big Man in moka *dress.*

publicly discussed, such messages from the supernatural often carry more weight than any actions and strategies Yombi might himself have devised.

As a leader, Yombi demonstrates a nearly uncanny ability to deal with the problems brought to his attention. Some disputes involve pigs and property. For instance, one man's pig destroys another man's garden. But the owner of the greedily devoured garden has failed to maintain his fence and must therefore assume responsibility for the gluttonous pig's access to its feast. Other disputes involve people and property. For instance, one man harvests the pandanus fruit of a second man without the latter's permission. Others involve men and women. One man's wife is accused of an adulterous affair with a younger unmarried man. Some involve co-wives. Any man with more than one wife is frequently forced to deal with inevitable jealousies and claims that he is showering his attentions disproportionately. Angry wives publicly transform his status from fair husband to instigator of domestic antagonism. Yombi is expected to exact justice from these disputes.

Unlike a Western court, with its litigants, lawyers, jurors and judges, Yombi operates with only the disputants and himself. He is less concerned with right and wrong and more concerned with balance. No winner, no loser, no one goes to jail. Like the international peace negotiations of 1991 in Cambodia and the Middle East, Imbonggu justice demands that everyone walk away with something, for any other outcome risks everyone walking away with nothing. Yombi's strategy often rests on his ability to speak for hours on the merits of both sides of a dispute. Sometimes it seems disputants merely walk away dazed, uncertain what (or even if) they have gained or lost. If neither party swings an axe at the other, the process has been a success. If spectators walk away, nodding in agreement, the process has been a success. Yombi's primary objective is to forge a compromise.

The construction of an acceptable compromise is more than a tribute to Yombi's skill as a jurist, however. Invariably, both parties to a dispute are members of his political following. Thus more is at stake than a dispute. From Yombi's perspective, what is at stake is nothing less than his political survival. To fail to achieve a compromise would be to risk forfeiting some amount of political support. A Big Man cannot afford right and wrong, winners and losers. In the tangled web of Imbonggu society, nearly every dispute eventually involves nearly everyone. Over several years, it was his ability to forge compromise in such situations that earned Yombi much of his following. He was seen as a man who could sort out what was truly important from what was merely emotional. Like the chess player who projects many moves ahead, he could envision the likely consequences of every possible outcome. His task was to convince the greatest number of people of the most desirable solution possible. He did so by resorting to his considerable oratorical and reasoning skills.

Skillful argument and persuasive presentation allow Yombi not only to resolve current disputes but to preempt similar ones in the future. In this sense he shapes village legal concepts in a manner comparable to the Western legal notion of precedent. Even apparently insignificant cases can be elevated to this Imbi equivalent of the Supreme Court. Yombi accepts jurisdiction over any case where he stands to gain advantage or that is so disruptive of village harmony that he has no option but to attempt to resolve it. In other cases, where a dispute seems incapable of resolution and where its impact is essentially limited to the disputants, Yombi often simply avoids the issue by decreeing that the disputants themselves should work it out. This strategy is particularly valuable in the case of domestic disputes between a man and a wife.

Not even the anthropologist fell beyond Yombi's legal stewardship. My anthropological cloak of participant observation provided no protection akin to diplomatic immunity. One day I found myself in the role of defendant in an Imbi lawsuit. This was very unfortunate, Yombi assured me. And he would have preferred things had not come to this. But the transgression was rather serious, after all. So Yombi, in his role as Imbonggu Judge Wapner, heard the issue of Kanambo v. The Anthropologist, or the Case of the Leaky Kitten. My accuser, twelve-year-old Kanambo, was one of the children who always gave me a wide berth and stared at me open-mouthed and bug-eyed from behind her mother's skirt. She was clearly uncertain what I might do to her but had heeded her mother's admonition that I was likely to one day consume a disrespectful Imbonggu child. And now, it seemed, I had indeed committed some offense against her. But as I sat down on the grass before my house, I had no idea what it was that I had done. Yombi talked for a long time about how I was a very good man. I did not bring alcohol into the village, although I was known to drink beer while playing tennis with Australians when we all should have been at church services. I shared my tobacco and kerosene. I read people the letters from their sons and daughters on the coast or in the big city of Port Moresby. I wrote out the dictated responses of the recipients of those letters, put stamps on them, and mailed them back to those same sons and daughters. I was a very good member of the village and everyone was very happy with my living there.

Yombi meekly admitted that he was even embarrassed that we were sitting on the grass dealing with such a minor dispute, but the insult to Kanambo was great, after all. The problem stemmed from an incident that had occurred several days earlier. Yombi had sought to mute the complaint, but without success. Kanambo had borrowed Beast, one of my two Siamese cats. Everyone in Tona had come to appreciate the skill and enthusiasm of Beast and Brute in tracking down, capturing, and devouring rats. Every house in the village had rats, but only my house had cats. It had become a common practice for young girls to come to my house in the evening and seek permission for Beast or Brute to spend the night with them. Since neither Beast nor Brute fully comprehended these negotiations or their obligations, I provided the girls a small amount of canned mackerel with which to lure the cats back to their houses. In the morning, the cats invariably returned to my house for their breakfast of mackerel. The girls eventually stopped by to tell me how much fun it had been having the cats spend the night. And, of course, the cats had managed to kill many rats. I came to feel like the proud parent of the two most popular and talented children in school.

But Kanambo's experience on this occasion had been less positive. Yombi explained that Kanambo had curled up for the night, Beast lying beside her on the floor. She soon fell asleep. Sometime later she awakened. She felt her side and the floor near her. They were both damp. Beast was no longer nearby. In the morning she told her mother of these events. The two of them drew for Yombi the inevitable conclusion, which he was forced to explain to me now. Beast had urinated on Kanambo. This was very unlikely, I argued. After all, Beast had been sleeping on my bed for months. He had also been sleeping in every house in the village for months. Not once had there been a complaint about his behavior, beyond the occasional confrontation with a dog or pig. In fact, I was deluged with requests from people inviting him to spend the night in their houses. True, admitted Yombi. And that made it all the more difficult to understand how Beast could have done such a thing. My defense seemed to have failed Beast on his day in court.

Yombi spoke forcefully on the offense to Kanambo, by coincidence his eldest daughter. She was clearly entitled to compensation for her suffering and humiliation. Her mother Alu had been forced to wash Kanambo's soiled *laplap,* a length of imported thin Chinese cotton cloth wrapped around the body. There was no way to save Kanambo's grass skirt. Alu had been forced to discard it. Alu would have to replace it at a cost of much time and energy obtaining grass and crafting a new skirt. Yombi then spoke eloquently of the previous good behavior of Beast and the invariable willingness of the anthropologist to observe the rules and conventions of village life. This was indeed an unfortunate situation. I expressed my sorrow that Kanambo had undergone her ordeal. Yombi wrapped up the proceeding by decreeing that I would pay compensation to Kanambo in the amount of two kina (approximately US$2.75 at the time). I accepted the decision and handed a two kina banknote to Kanambo, from whom it was immediately liberated by her mother Alu. In an effort to ward off any similar disputes in future, Yombi extended his decision to include the warning to all households in Tona that any future invitations for Beast to spend the night carried with them the host's implicit assumption of responsibility for any and all incidents of unwanted urination. I had been granted immunity from prosecution in the future, but Beast had suffered the indignity of being branded criminally incontinent.

But being an Imbonggu Big Man is much more than keeping the peace. A Big Man must demonstrate the capacity to stage successful ceremonial exchanges involving valued items of wealth. Those exchanges may involve amassing hundreds or thousands of pigs or kina (pearl) shells given publicly to recipients for the purpose of creating debt, satisfying a debt, or merely to demonstrate the economic and political superiority of donor over recipient. The Imbonggu call these occasions *moka,* both the activity and the word borrowed from the Melpa people to the northeast of Ialibu.

The Big Man is the principal organizer and master of ceremonies for *moka* (A. Strathern 1971). He seeks to entice followers to contribute valuables for the specific occasion, either by calling in old debts or by placing himself in debt with the promise of future repayment. On one occasion, a Big Man named Orei put together a *moka* involving nearly five hundred pigs made available to him by ninety-six of his followers. Some were pigs owed him in reciprocity for his earlier contributions to *moka* or brideprices. Others were pigs loaned to him against his promise of repayment. The amassed pigs then were given publicly by Orei to his counterpart from another clan and village.

The Big Man receiving Orei's gift was obligated to organize an even larger gift to be handed back to Orei at a later date, possibly in as much as five or six years.

A moka *ceremony involves the transfer of hundreds of pigs between competing groups; such events are orchestrated by Big Men.*

From that return gift, Orei would repay those supporters who had loaned him pigs earlier, and he would create new debts he could call in later by giving pigs to newer potential supporters. In this manner, Big Men from competing clans and villages were locked in competitive exchange relationships throughout their adult years. The ability to manage these exchanges to the economic benefit of supporters is one of the principal prerequisites to achieving the status of Big Man. A Big Man may be involved simultaneously in several such exchange relationships. I once watched a Big Man receive nearly five hundred slaughtered and cooked pigs. He and his ninety male supporters placed the meat on their backs and the backs of their wives and then immediately walked and ran nearly ten miles to hand it all over to a third Big Man and his followers that same afternoon. Such quick turnaround of assets is rare, but Big Men must be adept at disposing of such massive quantities of meat. Even three hundred hungry Imbonggu cannot consume literally tons of perishable meat in the two or three days before it rots. Big Men further demonstrate their skill by redistributing meat from where it is overly abundant to where it may be used to greatest advantage, both by the recipient and by the Big Man manipulating the system. The meat will eventually be eaten by some, provided at social and ceremonial gatherings such as for brideprice by others, or sold at market for cash by still others. By aligning themselves with a skilled Big Man, ordinary men reap their own benefits from a Big Man's successes.

On such large public exchange ceremonies, Big Men indeed give most of their apparent wealth away. In truth, of course, much of the wealth belongs to other people. The activity is somewhat analogous to brokers in the stock market. They

Big Men exchanging kina *shells and modern currency (also known as* kina*) at a* moka

turn over massive sums of wealth, taking commissions on individual transactions while ensuring that investors also realize profits from their participation. In a sense, Yombi was the Dean Witter of Nagop and Tona. The presentation of a public *moka* is a truly spectacular event. But in each exchange relationship, a *moka* may occur only every five or six years. And such occurrences will alternate between those in which a Big Man is the flamboyant donor of an impressively massive sum that must be reciprocated and those in which he is the humbled recipient of a sum of wealth that will tax all his skills to reciprocate. The public presentation of *moka* lasts only two or three days. The following five or six years are given over to the truly difficult work.

As the most recent donor in a *moka* relationship, a Big Man will expend a great deal of effort in demanding reciprocity within a reasonable period of time, partly to repay anxious supporters and partly to underwrite additional *moka* payments to still other Big Men. As the most recent recipient in a *moka* relationship, a Big Man must cajole and threaten his usual supporters as well as entice new supporters until he controls sufficient wealth to repay the previous gift. While he deals with the pressure of amassing the repayment, he must also fend off the pressure of others to make the return gift quickly. In something of a confidence game, Big Men must convince some men that they have so much wealth at their disposal that it is in their obvious best interests to get in on the scheme and share in the inevitable profits. At the same time a Big Man must convince other men that he borders on being destitute and all he needs is a little more time. He is the dashing and irresistible Big Man Trump with a cash-flow problem, or the lovable Imbonggu Wimpy who will gladly pay his Imbi Popeye on Tuesday for the hamburger today.

Like his counterparts among Western financiers, the Imbonggu Big Man must work his deals under intense scrutiny from competitors and the public at large. Thus one is always struck with the apparent contradiction that the Big Man is most often the man with the fewest pigs in the village. It is better to be seen with minimal assets in order to discourage one's creditors from demanding repayment. A Big Man's pigs are most likely in the care of a sister who is married and living in another village. At least temporarily they are at the disposal of her husband. Others will be dispersed among the brothers of a Big Man's wives. Still others will be donated to men in need of pigs for a son's brideprice. Another may be provided to a man who needs to sacrifice a pig to spirits to cure a sick family member. Other avenues of investment abound. All have in common the obligation to provide repayment when the Big Man demands it.

But if a Big Man is intent on hiding his wealth, other Big Men are equally intent on discovering it. Wives and sisters of Big Men are regularly pressed into service as agents of espionage. Their task is to monitor which women are looking after whose pigs and to pass that information back to their fathers and brothers. Imbonggu Big Men spend as much time walking the muddy brown paths of the Ialibu Basin visiting daughters and sisters to obtain this information as they do seeking to entice men to contribute to an upcoming *moka*. Big Men work untiringly at their craft. Andrew Strathern's documentary film (Granada Television International 1974) shows the efforts of Ongka to organize what the post-Gulf War generation of Americans would label "The Mother of All *Moka*." Ongka's relief and joy become palpable when he can finally claim control over the requisite number of pigs to stage the *moka* that will assure his place in Kawelka Big Man history.

But even within his own village, among his own followers, a Big Man is also subject to daily scrutiny by those who seek to press their own claims for repayment of a minor debt and by those who wish to feast uninvited at his table. I once asked Yombi why he spent several hours walking to the bush to cut firewood only to return with enough wood for two or three days when he could easily have cut and carried enough for a fortnight, assuming the occasional assistance of his sons. On a scale of value per mile, I calculated that Yombi's firewood was the most expensive in Tona. As I explained all this in detail, Yombi smiled and nodded his head in agreement. Alas, that was yet another price of being wealthy and powerful. After all, he explained, if he were to pile up a large supply of firewood under the eaves of his house, it would be obvious to all who passed that he was preparing to kill, cook, and distribute a large number of pigs. Everyone in the village would instantly be at his door reminding him of the day they had loaned him some insignificant thing or hoping to convince him that their need for pig meat was greater than his own. No, he concluded, it was easier to walk to the bush every second day than to fend off such demands and pleas. The life of a Big Man is not as soft as it seems.

15 / Human Victims in a World of Sorcerers

"Kondoli, if you must go to his house, be sure you do not eat his food. He is a sorcerer and he will kill you." This was the usual farewell instruction whenever I left Tona to meet with a man in a different village. This advice reflected the chronic levels of fear and paranoia experienced by the Imbi in their interactions with outsiders, who were by definition enemies and strangers. The fear that sorcerers delivered their poisonous concoctions by mixing them with food was widespread. Such poisons made one ill. They could even lead to death. The paranoid belief that one was the object of sorcery was shared by all adult men.

The Imbi live in a harsh world. That harshness extends beyond the cold and damp mist engulfing the village for days at a time. The social climate is equally harsh. Each group of patrilineally related Imbonggu men, including the Imbi, is an island refuge in a hostile sea of enemies. Men are safest when they are at home, although even there the risks to health and life are great indeed. But to leave one's patrilineal refuge and venture forth into a world of enemies, sorcerers, and spirits causes even the bravest Imbonggu to take extreme precautions. Hence the invariable warning to refrain from accepting food and tobacco when offered by non-Imbi men. The reasons for this pervasive hostility and consequent suspicion are in no way extraordinary. The causes lie in the common events of daily life and social interaction. Men seek revenge for any of a multitude of reasons: a perceived insult, the theft of property (especially pigs), the adulterous affairs of wives, the inability to recover pigs or money owed them, or events and incidents that seem personally directed at them.

Men may experience the aggression of sorcerers firsthand, as when they are ill or in pain. A man may also experience the effects of sorcery indirectly when it is aimed at one of his children or one of his pigs, causing either to become ill or to sustain an injury. By contrast, a wife is seldom victimized in this way by sorcerers seeking vengeance against her husband. An enemy prior to marriage, she continues to be an enemy after moving to her husband's village. A wife (especially a younger one) is more likely to be thought of as the means by which a sorcerer's poison is administered to his victim. Whenever a man's illness is attributed to sorcery, his wife becomes a suspect. There is invariably suspicion that she tainted her husband's meal with poison, possibly on behalf of her angry father or brother. Or possibly she engaged a sorcerer to attack an overly abusive husband. In rare cases where a woman is thought to be the victim of sorcery, it is assumed she is the victim of her husband's relatives rather than his enemies. After all, she is one of the latter.

Few grievances by themselves are sufficient to seek to kill a man. Most individual grievances are minor. It is normally the accumulation of unresolved antagonisms that leads to the attempt to actually kill the victim. More often, the object is to encourage the victim to seek out the sorcerer and attempt to reach a compromise by which a spell can be reversed or a pattern of aggressive sorcery can be terminated. Illness implies that someone is angry with the victim. It sends the clear message that some situation must be corrected.

The search for a sorcerer or his client is not as complicated and difficult as it might appear. Men are normally aware of which enemies harbor grudges. The circulation of rumor and gossip is extremely efficient in terms of both speed and distance. Men are also normally aware of the specific nature of a grievance, as well as the range of options available for its resolution. If the identity of the aggressor is clear (or at least accepted as such), the victim may approach him directly or through an intermediary. Both sides then negotiate a strategy whereby the victim makes amends and the sorcerer ceases his aggressive action.

Where the identity of the sorcerer or his client is unclear, an identity can be ascertained by various means. Illness that manifests itself in vomiting is a clear sign that one has been the target of sorcery. A specialist in the art of interpreting stomach contents is called in. By examining the items expelled from the victim's stomach, such a specialist can figure out which item contained the poisonous additive. The memory of the victim fills out the puzzle by recalling the source of the tainted food. "Kondoli, if you go to his house, be sure you do not eat his food. He will try to kill you."

Less commonly employed since the arrival of Christian missionaries is direct communication with spirits in an effort to obtain such critical information. In the past, the Imbonggu met directly with spirits in special structures, known as dream houses, that dotted the landscape. By 1975, only a handful remained. They were normally located in nearly inaccessible places deep in the forest or perched precariously on steep mountainsides. A dream house may be the abode of spirits, but it is under the custodial care of the men on whose land it is situated. A man in desperate need of information that might be gained only from the spirits arranges to spend an evening in the dream house. In the past, access was secured by the payment of a small pig or shell to the landholder. In more recent times the price of admission has become a frozen chicken or the equivalent of a few dollars in cash. On arriving at the dream house, the guest addresses the spirits. The conflict situation is spelled out in as complete detail as possible. The exact nature of the information sought, such as a location or the name of a person, is also set out. The man seeking the aid of the spirits is accompanied by a friend or relative. After informing the spirits about the purpose of the visit, the two guests prepare a meal for themselves. Some of the meat, usually pig or chicken, is given as an offering to the spirits. The man seeking the spirits' aid sleeps. His comrade assumes the critical role of observer. He must remain awake throughout the night and observe the movements of his sleeping friend. In the morning, the sleeper will recount the events of his dreams, for it is through those dreams that the spirits answer his questions and provide the information he seeks. The second man recounts the movements of his sleeping partner. The two bits of information are put together and interpreted, either by the two men themselves or by a third man if neither dreamer nor friend is skilled in doing so. The interpretation of the dreams and sleeping movements contains the information the dreamer seeks. Once the information is understood, the victim is in a position to approach the sorcerer and seek to resolve the conflict between them.

The Imbi are surrounded by sorcerers. They stress that although all their neighbors are sorcerers, they themselves are not. In fairness to their neighbors, however, it must be noted that all the neighbors of the Imbi claim that the Imbi are actually among the most lethal sorcerers in the Ialibu Basin. By contrast, each neighboring group proclaims their own innocence of the charge and their complete ignorance of the sorts of activities practiced by sorcerers. Thus the Imbi, like all their neighbors, see themselves as an island of vulnerable victims surrounded by dangerous sorcerers. Fear and paranoia are two predictable consequences. "Billio, do not smoke his tobacco if he offers it to you. He will try to kill you." But there is an even more fascinating possibility: Can an anthropologist kill by sorcery?

Yala was a constant source of information and amusement early in my stay in Tona. He visited my house each morning, led me around the village and gardens and into the bush each day, and joined me again at my hearth each evening. He never asked me for anything. Rather, he seemed genuinely curious about me. In his own way he was observing me as thoroughly as I was observing him. Yala was keenly interested in *masta*. One day he and I accompanied Nabene and Bepi to Nabene's garden on the slopes of Mount Ialibu. Nabene's husband Turi was also part of the expedition. Turi and Yala had felled a tree some months before to make way for Nabene's garden. It was time to return to the tree and chop it up for firewood.

When we reached Nabene's garden, I stationed myself at the top of the slope overlooking the plot. I set about sketching its outline and mapping the locations of the various vegetables planted in it. Further down the hill, Nabene and Bepi harvested vegetables for the evening meal. At the base of the slope, Yala and Turi carefully dismantled the tree with their axes. After several minutes, Yala scrambled up the slope to where I was sitting, joined now by Nabene and Bepi. He unfolded a large leaf and spread it on the ground before us. Bepi and Nabene offered approving smiles. I immediately felt uneasy. The leaf was alive, or at least its contents were. I stared at a pile of several dozen squirming grubs, each the size of my thumb or larger. They were the reason for Yala's extraordinary care in chopping the tree into bits of firewood. Eggs deposited in the tree months before had metamorphosed within the tree. Their life-style seemed unexciting and devoid of freedom. Eating and growth were synonymous in the life cycle of these fat little creatures. As they ate the tree, their little bodies swelled to fill the very space they had created at their last meal. After such a short, dull life, there was little to cheer at upon their emergence into sunlight for the first time. If eating had been the essence of the life behind them, eating would be the essence of the short life left to them as well. But their days as eaters were ended. No longer eaters, they had become eatees. From diner to dinner. What a difference an *n* makes! I came to feel increasingly uneasy.

After much muffled conversation and numerous gestures in my direction, Nabene showed me a carefully selected grub. With a smile and small giggle, she

Bepi with her daughter Toea, who demonstrates the technique for eating grubs

dropped the poor creature into a small fire Yala had started. In a few seconds, a distinctly audible popping sound signaled that the creature was now food. Along with three others he was removed from the fire. Yala, Bepi, and Nabene each took one. The fourth was handed to me by Nabene, whose smile was even larger now. The other three each took a turn at demonstrating the proper technique for consuming the now brownish snack. Their eyes fixed on me as I contemplated my options. I had heard from every anthropologist of my acquaintance that something like this would eventually happen to me. The moment of truth was clearly at hand. I could refuse the grub with as much sincerity and politeness as I could muster, but this would almost certainly give offense. At the very least it would provide public evidence that in the final analysis I was only an outsider. As I mulled over my limited options, each with its own disadvantages, Nabene began to laugh. Yala demonstrated the eating technique a second time. It was now or never. I placed the grub in my mouth, willing my tongue and throat to permit its passage. Fearing an attack of acute nausea, I began furiously to convince myself that I had eaten a normal snack that was in no way exceptional. The fiction worked.

Nabene and Bepi nodded approvingly and turned their stares to Yala. I only half heard their claims to him that they had known all along I would eat it. Yala seemed unconvinced. A few moments later, he offered a second grub. I accepted it but delayed eating it right away. I hoped instead that some roar would emanate from the mountain. Then, while my friends' attention was focused on discovering the origin of the noise, I could ungratefully toss the grub into the forest. Luck was not with me. After a few moments I found myself again eyeball to eyeball with Yala. He was beginning to smile, clearly on the brink of offering an "I told you so" to Nabene and Bepi. I ate the second grub.

Inevitably, I was soon offered a third grub by Nabene, who was now operating under the unfortunate delusion that I did indeed find the snack enjoyable. Having already eaten two, and thereby having demonstrated my good faith, it now seemed possible to reject the offer. Yala was not about to grant any such concession, however. "I knew you did not like our food. You are just like all the other white men. You do not like Imbonggu food." I protested weakly that I had already eaten some grubs, two of the beasts surely permitting use of the plural. I was merely satisfied and no longer hungry. Yala persisted in his accusation that I did not like Imbonggu food. The obvious tactic seemed to be to take the offensive, to fight fire with fire. I challenged Yala with the speculation that there were probably several European foods he would not be particularly fond of. "No," he assured me, "I like all European foods." The challenge was clear. As we returned to Tona, I invited Yala to come to my house that evening for some European food he would not like. Poor Yala was now trapped. He could not back down in the witnessing presence of Nabene and Bepi.

Some distance from Ialibu is a place known as Det. All I knew of Det at the time was that Father Sam, a Catholic priest, served a parish there. One of his many ventures included the growing of small, red chili peppers. They were grown as a cash crop in an effort to support the efforts of the mission. Father Sam regularly sent large plastic containers of dried peppers to his colleagues at the Ialibu Catholic mission station. Some of those peppers made their way to a Peace Corps couple,

Bob and Sandy Vogel. Through them, a large jar made its way to me in Tona village. The aging that occurred during this circuitous route was unnecessary to the chilies. They began the journey as the hottest chilies I had eaten before sampling those of Thailand several years later. Indeed, hot seems an inadequate adjective. Corrosive might well be more accurate.

That evening Nabene and Bepi arrived at my house with their husbands. Gradually, several others arrived, all intent on sharing Yala's windfall European food. Finally, Yala entered my house and took a seat at my hearth. Conversation eventually shifted from my *Sports Illustrated* magazines to the subject of food. Our afternoon grub snack session was recalled, and Nabene proclaimed to everyone that I was the only white man in her experience to eat grubs. Everyone was impressed. Bepi casually reminded me that I had promised Yala some European food. In one final effort to avoid catastrophe, I explained that this food was very good for some Europeans, but many did not like it. Yala restated his firm conviction that he liked all European foods. Once again he noted that I did not really like Imbonggu food, as evidenced by my refusal to continue eating grubs that afternoon.

There was no easy way out. I took one of the small dried peppers, placed it in my mouth, and chewed it. Years of regular dining at a small Mexican restaurant specializing in hot chili sauce had conditioned my ability to consume such peppers raw. Yala lacked such intense, sustained training. Eager to make his point, he placed a pepper in his mouth. He raised his eyebrows and cocked his head casually to the side as if to register his view that this small item had no taste at all. But as all eyes remained fixed on him, his eyebrows raised even higher. As they continued to ascend his forehead, his eyes became incredibly larger. He presented such a powerful facial expression that spectators themselves experienced enlargement of their own eyes as if they were physically connected to Yala's. The house was deathly quiet. Yala's mouth opened wide. He gasped and took several deep breaths. He commenced a futile fanning of his mouth with a frantic hand. Tears streamed down his cheeks. All eyes followed him as he rose to his feet and raced from the house. People looked at the door through which Yala had fled the house. They looked at one another, then at me. Several people at once raced from the house in pursuit of Yala. Others remained seated and speculated on what they had witnessed. No one asked to inspect one of my peppers, however.

After a few minutes, several children returned to the house. They described how Yala had raced across the village and down the muddy, rock-strewn path to the small stream below Tona. He had thrown water in his mouth, even submerged his entire head in the freezing stream. But there was no relief. He told them his mouth burned with a fierceness he had never experienced. He feared he was dying. I assured everyone that he would not die, and that the discomfort would eventually disappear. Several minutes later, Yala returned to the house. The pain had subsided but had not disappeared entirely. He tried to explain the phenomenon for his listeners. It was clear that he could not do so adequately. People began to reenact his behavior for Yala. Laughter broke out as each new comic imitation was offered up. Yala took it all well. When he departed for the evening, he assured everyone that he was recovered and would not die.

Yala and the chili pepper continued to be the hot topic of conversation in my house for several evenings. Several days later, Yala showed up at my house, another young man in tow. Without a hint that anything was amiss, he announced, "Kondoli, Manda wishes to try your food." No one else offered a gasp or giggle. It was clear that all were party to the joke and that poor Manda had been set up. I tried my best to assure Manda that he would not like the food. I resorted to lying by noting that my supply was low. This merely served to produce the inevitable complaint that I was guilty of hoarding and did not want to share my food with my Imbonggu friends. I was trapped. Reluctantly, I handed Manda a single chili. Usurping my earlier role, Yala explained to Manda that the food was to be chewed slowly rather than swallowed immediately. Manda, of course, proceeded to offer a reasonable reenactment of Yala's performance of a few evenings before. As his suffering mounted and seemed on the verge of transforming itself into fear, several children escorted him to the stream for relief. They soon returned to a house filled with people still laughing at Manda's distress. He was treated to the customary reenactment of his torment.

I went to bed fearing that I had done something that might well result in disaster. First, of course, there was the nagging sense that what I had done was somehow inherently wrong and cruel. My concern then shifted to fear that people might avoid me, thereby thwarting my anthropological effort to come to know the Imbi. Had I acted in such a way that the Imbonggu would dislike me? The next few days were stressful. But I came to learn, as most anthropologists do, that doing something outrageous or foolish does not inevitably lead to disaster. In fact, the opposite seems more often to be true. This incident did much to facilitate my acceptance in the village and among the residents of nearby villages. Fortunately, no one held a grudge. Nor did anyone suffer damage beyond a temporarily bruised ego. One particularly memorable victim was Tongei, a boy of approximately twelve years of age. As his suffering diminished, he pleaded, "If you want to kill me, just kill me!" I wondered if he would warn all future visitors to my house, "Do not eat Kondoli's food if he offers it to you. He will try to kill you."

Alas, even among the Imbonggu, all good things must end. I had been in Tona for eighteen months when Anakali returned from a lengthy stint of plantation labor on the island of New Britain. The chili pepper routine ended one memorable evening within days of his return to Tona. He had returned to the village to obtain a wife, establish his pig herd, and stake out his favored garden plots. In an effort to acquire his wife, he had visited with Wakea, whose love magic was universally accepted as the most potent in the village. After all, the evidence of eighty-year-old Wakea married to an eighteen-year-old wife (his third) was all the proof required. Wakea provided Anakali with some fresh green ginger he was to eat prior to meeting with his future wife. Anakali consumed the entire supply of fresh ginger with enthusiasm. Sadly, an hour later he added to it one of Father Sam's chili peppers. The lethal mix was more than poor Anakali's stomach could bear. After the usual routine, Anakali improvised by lying down in his house, vomiting, and generally giving every appearance of imminent mortality. All agreed this latest performance had gone terribly wrong. But why?

Anakali's condition appeared to worsen. I was asked to give him some of my medicine. After all, it was I who had poisoned him. I replied weakly that the problem was no doubt the combination of one small chili pepper and a rather large quantity of green ginger. My medicine would do him no good and might even do some harm. His mother and sisters began to cry. Others joined in the wailing. The rumor that Anakali was dying flashed through the village. Someone must have committed sorcery against Anakali. But who? And why? I nervously stayed awake through the night as the mourning and wailing continued. By mid-morning, Anakali was sitting up, well along the road to recovery. During the night he vomited. One of the men inspected the contents of his stomach and found only the ginger and the chili pepper. It was agreed that Wakea could hardly commit sorcery through his love magic known to all the men. It was also agreed that Kondoli (the anthropologist) would not commit sorcery. And the chili peppers were known to do no more than produce mild discomfort. It was concluded that the two items, both obviously powerful, had combined badly in Anakali's stomach. Sorcery was no longer suspected. Still, Anakali had indeed experienced significant distress. Wakea's love magic had never been known to cause any such ill effects, whereas the chili peppers were offered to unsuspecting victims for precisely that purpose. It was obvious that if there were any fault, it lay with me. I would have to compensate Anakali with two kina in cash. To avoid further repetitions, I refused to dispense chili peppers in the future. The fact that Anakali had been the victim was in a sense quite fortunate. Had it been a young man from another village, the charges of sorcery might have produced a much more tense and difficult situation. It seems even anthropologists can kill.

16 / "Living like a White Man"

With the first administrative patrols by the Australian colonial government into the Ialibu Basin, there began an irreversible process of change in the lives and society of the Imbonggu. A familiar world of people and spirits was invaded by unimaginably new and different creatures. They were tall, white, demanding, greedy, and otherwise incomprehensible. Fifty years later they remain largely a mystery to the Imbonggu. Until I took up residence in Tona, the Imbi's direct experience of white foreigners was limited to occasional visits by Australian patrol officers, health workers, and Christian missionaries. Each came to the village for a specific purpose. Those visits produced demands for money, labor, and the abandonment of traditional culture. In their wake they left anger, frustration, a sense of loss, and puzzlement at the purpose of it all.

Early interaction between Imbonggu and foreigners was limited to the domestic sphere. A few Imbonggu became servants, cooks, cleaners, and gardeners. As religious converts, they were servants to the Lord and his missionaries. As paid laborers, they worked hard and long for cash that was then extracted from them through tax levies. Socially, there was virtually no interaction between Imbonggu and the colonial intruders. At the end of the day, Imbonggu left the government's administrative post at Ialibu and returned to their villages. Other Papua New Guineans in the government's employ made their way to the end of the government station where the low-covenant housing (low-cost, small, lacking plumbing) was located. The expatriate Australian officers retired to the opposite end of the station where their high-covenant houses (high-cost, large, with plumbing facilities) were situated. Missionaries retired to their individual mission stations, Catholics here, Lutherans there, Baptists somewhere else. In much the same way as the Imbonggu return to their homes in the dark to avoid contact with ghosts and spirits, *masta* fled to their enclaves at the end of the day in order to avoid prolonged interaction with New Guineans and to preserve their sense of themselves as superior outsiders charged with their various missions to save and improve the deprived and depraved Imbonggu. Cultures at war during the day. Cultures in retreat at night.

Despite the limited interaction between Imbonggu and outsiders, each displayed a constant curiosity about what the other was doing. I found myself in the position of being one of the primary links between the two camps. Imbonggu bombarded me with questions and complaints about *masta,* who in turn bombarded me with questions and complaints about *oli* (a derogatory term applied to New Guineans by Australian colonial officers). And, of course, each had questions and complaints about my interaction with the other. When I agreed with a government position, I was a traitor to the Imbi. When I took the side of the Imbonggu, I was a traitor to the

Ialibu government station; this expatriate enclave included large houses, a tennis court, and the Royal Ialibu Yacht Club.

white outsiders. This position between the two groups was often unpleasant but always enlightening. It opened my eyes to the wider world in which the Imbonggu live and to some of the pressures of modernity to which they daily are forced to respond.

At the same time, I cannot deny that I enjoyed spending time with the expatriate population at Ialibu. The Australian and American teachers, government officers, and volunteers were a collection of interesting, often charming, characters. As among the Imbonggu, I made many friendships I cherish deeply. Many of those colonial officers and teachers have visited me in America, and I have visited some of them in Australia. Most anthropologists find themselves in the position of being dependent on people whom they would prefer not to be. Those relationships may occasionally shape the nature of fieldwork, yet they are normally excluded from the bulk of anthropological literature. In his classic book *Argonauts of the Western Pacific,* Bronislaw Malinowski (1922:6) issued the anthropological commandment that we must avoid all contact with other foreigners. Interesting advice in light of the revelations that appeared in his diary notes published later (Malinowski 1967).

I chose to maintain contact with as many of the elements of the cultural and social landscape of Ialibu as I could. I looked forward to enjoying a cold beer and talking baseball with members of the Capuchin Friars' Mission, especially those who came from Pittsburgh. As a graduate student at Pitt, I spent many days and nights watching the Pirates play baseball in Three Rivers Stadium. The Mendi Catholic diocese boasted an airmail subscription to *The Sporting News,* which brought box scores to Pirates fans a world away on a weekly basis. Invariably, I found the Catholic missionaries of my acquaintance to be deeply concerned with the welfare of the Imbonggu and very well informed about Imbonggu culture and society. While the Catholic missionaries were tolerant in the extreme, their various protestant counterparts enjoyed tolerance in significantly reduced quantity. That fact led to a degree of friction between me and them that diminished my attempts to seek interaction and companionship with the non-Catholic community.

The Australian and American government officers and teachers offered a congenial and often boisterous community where I could maintain links to my own cultural underpinnings. On Friday of each week, this group convened at the Royal Ialibu Yacht Club for a communal dinner, followed by darts and that other Australian pastime—beer drinking. While I was accepted as a member in good standing of the Royal Ialibu Yacht Club, there seemed always to be some doubt as to whether or not I would attend these weekly sessions. Each week a special invitation was extended to me. It took a form that never changed but became increasing bizarre as the months and years wore on. And, of course, it betrayed much about the prevailing state of interaction between expatriates and Imbonggu. "Willy, come down from the village and live like a white man tonight."

Living like a white man was a fascinating experience in a variety of ways. For me, it meant primarily playing darts, drinking beer, discussing international politics, listening to sporting events via shortwave radio reception, and discussing the local and national events of contemporary Papua New Guinea. Initially, one of my primary activities was defending American society and politics to Australians for whom American politics and society were nonsensical. Did I own a gun and had I ever shot anyone? After all, this seemed like an American national pastime to Australians. Had I voted for Richard Nixon, and even if I had not, why had so many Americans done so? The man was not well thought of by the Australians of my acquaintance. At the same time, what was the point of the Watergate hearings? Only Americans could devote so much time and money to something so truly insignificant as political bugging. After all, spying is just another quirky American pastime.

We listened to Wimbledon tennis matches in Jimmy Connors' heyday; the classic cricket struggles for The Ashes, dominated by Australia's Chappell brothers; Aussie rules football from Melbourne; and rugby league from Sydney. My efforts to promote America's baseball World Series met with the customary questions about American arrogance in our insistence on calling our championship teams "World Champions" when they play games no one else plays (American football) or when they play none of the other nations who play the same games (baseball and basketball). The defeat of an American tennis player by an Australian tennis star was always cause for celebration. Did everyone in America really like "gridiron"? The game was nothing more than a modified version of rugby turned soft by mountains of equipment and made boring by the apparent inability of its players to think and run at the same time. The concept of the huddle left Australians dumbfounded. Equally amazing was the American institution of the cheerleader. Why was it necessary to create fan enthusiasm? Cheerleaders were nothing more than the athletic equivalent of television stage managers holding signs aloft so the studio audience might know when to clap their hands.

I spent two years pleading with my fellow Yacht Club members to join me in listening to a college football game via shortwave at four o'clock in the morning. Finally, after a night of particularly convivial drinking, we all settled down to listen to what I assured them was a big game involving Notre Dame. I explained the position of Notre Dame in the American football hierarchy, the significance of this particular game for the weekly polls, and everything else I could think of to highlight the importance of the game. The broadcast began with the traditional setting of the stage by the announcers. The Irish emerged from their locker room to an awesome crowd roar. We could barely hear the announcers above the din. Yet they continued to set the stage. Inevitably coming to the subject of cheerleaders, the announcers proclaimed for any Australians who happened to be listening, "On the sidelines, the cheerleaders are rooting for the Irish." That was the last broadcast word we heard as the Aussies collapsed into howling laughter. For Australians the word "root" is synonymous with sexual intercourse.

My living like a white man was an equally fascinating experience for the Imbonggu who knew me. It provided them with an accessible informant who was actually involved in some very bizarre activities. The drinking sessions were legendary to Imbonggu, who most often heard of them from friends and relatives working as domestic servants in Australian households. Other activities were more generally observable. Tennis, for instance. Wherever Australians went in the colonial development of Papua New Guinea, they left tennis courts in their wake. To say that tennis is a national passion in Australia is not an overstatement. It was the ideal game for the far-flung outposts of the colonial administration. The game requires only two players and minimal equipment. Courts were built throughout the nation by Papua New Guineans who lacked even the most vague understanding of their purpose. The spectacle of two Australians chasing a ball around such courts was a constant source of amazement and amusement to the Imbonggu. One of the things that most fascinated them was that, barring rain, the game was invariably underway Sunday morning as Imbonggu made their way to church services. It was still underway when those same Imbonggu emerged from church. The game itself was less interesting than the question of why all the white people except the missionaries played the game instead of attending church. I was frequently warned that God was probably quite angry about my preference for tennis over worship on Sunday mornings. But back in the village, the deeper question emerged. If some white men were so convinced that God demanded worship, then why were other white men so obviously unconvinced? One of the constant trials of living with the Imbonggu was attempting to avoid passing judgment on the work and beliefs of missionaries. Nevertheless, the question arises as to how much of himself or herself an anthropologist must forfeit in the pursuit of field research. My answer was that, while I sought to dig as deep as possible into the lives of Imbonggu to learn their beliefs and values, I could hardly seek to conceal my own beliefs, values, likes, and dislikes from them. Sincerity, contradiction, and confusion often go hand in hand in life. I would give the Imbonggu their opportunity to observe and question me. They never shrank from such opportunities. While they were pleased at my attempts to live like them, they were equally excited at the opportunity to probe my own experiences and culture as a means of understanding those perpetually enigmatic expatriates living only a few kilometers away.

Randy Bollig, a regular visitor, was a great favorite with the children, who asked him what time it was every two minutes. Here he is visiting with The Beast, alias the Leaky Kitten.

I often felt like a human pinball being banged from one informant to another by one informant or another, while all the time myself being an informant to one group or the other. But all this activity was rewarding not only in terms of my ability to collect the data that would provide me the most complete grasp of the interaction within and between these disparate communities, but also in terms of some successes with my efforts to reconcile the largely different worlds and experiences of my two communities. Randy Bollig, an American teacher at the high school, stayed with me several times in the village and became a favorite of the children there. He was host to occasional tour groups of Imbonggu intent on seeing the inside of a European's house. When I agreed to assist Peni in selling *laplap* at the local market so she could earn some money of her own, we were further aided by Anne Cowper, whose husband was advisor to the Ialibu Local Government Council. She cut thirty meters of cloth into pieces one meter in length. Anne then mystified Peni by stitching up the ends with a sewing machine whirring away atop her dining room table. Such moments were intensely satisfying, and it was easy to forget that the boundaries between expatriate and Imbonggu remained in place just beyond our small stage.

17 / Imbonggu Ethnographers

A persistent debate occurs among anthropologists about the basic nature of our research as an activity. The most vocal position decries research as exploitative in nature, stating that the anthropologist benefits disproportionately and that the informant population loses something in the exchange. After all, the anthropologist earns a Ph.D. or authors a book or articles. He or she may even earn a salary raise after several years of successful research and writing. By contrast, the argument goes, the people we study and write about gain nothing. No Ph.D., no book royalties, no movie rights, no revenues from the video cassette sales, or no assorted other phantom benefits.

On the other side of the debate is the argument that the Imbonggu, for example, gain exactly the same sorts of things the anthropologist does in the activity of fieldwork. That is, rewards of value as defined by local standards and aspirations. Such, after all, is the essence of exchange. Informants provide information for researchers, who provide other commodities in return. Commodities such as material goods and money, services such as transportation, and even comparable information about the culture of the anthropologist. The value of such information is not to be underestimated where its possession affords an informant the opportunity to assume a broker role between competing social or political groups. It is almost inconceivable that an anthropologist could be successful in field research if he or she refused to meet the basic expectations of reciprocity held by informants.

The Imbonggu assigned many roles to me. I was ogre to misbehaving children, potential husband and son-in-law, provider of tax payments, provider of transportation, provider of material goods, intermediary in cases of misunderstanding with government officials, and informant concerning the ways of white men (which required a great deal of explanation in the minds of my Imbi companions). I wrote letters for illiterate parents to their children in faraway places. I read and translated the responses from those same children. I translated and explained court summons papers and other legal documents. These were things of immediate value and benefit to the Imbi. Mutual benefit was the basis of our relationship. Those benefits differed in the way that Western financial transactions involve commodities usually quite different in nature. Americans exchange money for goods and services more often than they exchange money for money. An acceptable level of equivalence is defined, not by any inherent value of the commodities exchanged, but rather by perceived values in a specific place at a specific time. One dollar is worth one gallon of gasoline here, today. It is worth something more or less at a different location tomorrow, or even today. We negotiate today what we realize we want and need today or project we will want or need in the future. The Imbonggu view transactions exactly the same way and are every bit as adept at negotiating them.

Imbonggu served as my informants when it was convenient for them. They talked about issues on which they were individually informed and interested. Like many Americans, they also chose occasionally to talk about issues on which they were uninformed. And no doubt, on some occasions they talked about things not out of interest but out of the need to procure some good or service from the anthropologist. Often it was an Imbonggu who initiated interview sessions on topics known to be of interest to me or on topics it was hoped might become of interest to me. The purpose seldom appeared to be to provide an opportunity for my continued exploitation of informants. Rather, the purpose was the gentle but undeniable exploitation of the anthropologist by an informant!

So what was of interest to Imbonggu informants about a culture from the other side of the world? a culture embodied in a single representative living in Tona by little more than sheer chance on his part and crafty manipulation on the part of the Imbi themselves? Some things were to be predicted as obvious. My skin was a source of constant fascination. Frightened children watched as their curious mothers stroked my arms in an apparent effort to see if my color would rub off. More accurately, it was my lack of color that generated notice. It was even enshrined in my name. "Kondoli" was a variant of the word for the color red. Of all the colors on the Imbonggu palette, no label seemed closer to my pasty hue than red. The name was not a reflection of an Imbonggu tendency toward color blindness, but rather an artifact of my position beyond the normal range of their color spectrum. If I was close to anything in color, it was the yellowish mud worn by mourners at the death of a relative, an inappropriate name for even the most bizarre person. My bulk was another topic of considerable interest. While shorter than eight of the nine Australian administrative officers present at Ialibu during my stay, I was nevertheless taller than every living Imbonggu of my acquaintance, occasionally by truly astonishing differences. The Imbonggu are generally short of stature and are truly impressed at people taller than six feet. Much of my material culture inventory was also of general interest. My camera was always a mystery in its ability to produce likenesses of people. My tape recorder was fascinating in its ability to trap voices and save them for the future. Prior to my leaving for New Guinea, my parents gave me a gift that proved not only useful in recording field notes but also in entertaining my informants. The item was a ballpoint pen with a small light bulb in its tip that allowed me to write field notes in the dark. Word of this marvelous device spread through students at the local high school with the result that, whenever I found myself in a Ialibu village other than Tona, the children would demand I write something in the dark with my pen.

But Imbonggu interest in me went far beyond the superficial topics of my body and my material culture. About six months after I arrived in Tona, my surface mail subscription to *Sports Illustrated* began to arrive weekly, or more often monthly in bundles. One issue arrived sporting no mailing label whatsoever, bearing witness to the interest the magazine generated in the postal service. It was probably the only subscription to pass through the postal system, and its destination was no mystery. My attempts to explain the intricacies of the games illustrated in the magazine were largely unsuccessful. Gridiron was fascinating largely for the layers of equipment worn by its players. Body-building was fascinating for the layers of muscles worn by its devotees. Swimming, especially women's, was fascinating for the lack of body covering. Imbonggu were convinced that white women must be quite ugly under all the layers of clothing. Imbonggu stared in mute amazement at pasty white female missionaries wearing high collars, long sleeves, and long skirts in the heat of the afternoon. Bikini advertisements were enthusiastically studied by both male and female informants. I also subscribed to *Time* and *Newsweek,* both of which routinely contained photographs showing towering urban buildings that were a source of amazement, as were photographs of high technology, such as manufacturing, television, and medicine. I spent hours at a time explaining the contexts of such photographs.

But the greatest curiosity was aroused by advertisements. Still photos of bizarre people doing truly bizarre things. Tona ethnographers were quick to note many of the staples of American advertising. For instance, the apparent requirement that an ad include a beautiful woman, regardless of the commodity being advertised. Did only women drive cars in America? Clothing styles also stood out. Was it really necessary for men to wear tuxedos to drink whiskey? And why didn't the Australians and the anthropologists wear something more than jeans or shorts when they drank alcohol? Did all Americans live in huge houses with very beautiful furniture? Why did Americans always smile when they smoked cigarettes? Why were the people in the advertisements always so slim, whereas the tourists visiting Mount Hagen were always so fat? It often occurred to me that the Imbonggu were more aware of the subliminal messages of American advertising than were Americans.

The anthropologist with male informants; they also proved adept at playing the role of anthropologist with me as their primary informant.

American culture was subsumed under the heading "European," which encompassed Australians, New Zealanders, British, and Canadians equally. Imbonggu detected accent differences in radical cases and felt that Americans were generally more friendly toward them than were Australians, but beyond those differences the Europeans were interchangeable. No significant cultural distinctions were obvious to the Imbonggu. But differences between Europeans and Imbonggu abounded. Some defied explanation no matter how detailed or extended. For instance, why did European men work while their wives stayed at home and did nothing at all? Many Europeans did not even have children to care for, and when they did have children they seldom had more than two or three. They hired Imbonggu women to cook, do laundry, and clean their houses. What exactly did these white women do? And why did their husbands not put a stop to it and make the women work like Imbonggu men demanded of their wives? It was obvious that the lack of work and exercise had taken a physical toll. European women were seen as either scrawny or fat but seldom as physically fit and strong. Weak and unproductive, such women held little appeal for Imbonggu men. All these complaints aside, why did European men insist on having only one wife? Given their inability to bear large families, it was clear that many wives were necessary. Yet white men apparently failed to recognize the need or chose to do nothing about it. It was widely rumored that European men had sex with each other's wives and that fights resulted from it. Why would men fight over women when they could solve the problem by marrying several?

Why did some Europeans believe in God while others did not? Which ones were right? No Bishop Berkeley among the Imbonggu, the existence of God must be absolute and in no way dependent on the beliefs and perceptions of individuals. So which Europeans should the Imbonggu believe? After all, they had no direct knowledge of God's existence. Verbal disagreements between missionaries and other Europeans were witnessed with incredulity. Would the nonbelievers be struck dead? Europeans used profanity with ease, particularly on the tennis court, with no apparent concern for the dire consequences that Imbonggu were led to believe were inevitable. Only exceptional Europeans ever attended worship services or Bible study groups at the missions.

Like me, the Imbonggu were deeply interested in the interaction between Imbonggu and European. The basics of that interaction were without mystery. Europeans were in charge. They held all the good jobs with the government. They earned the highest salaries. They lived in the best houses and drove the expensive vehicles. They "thumped" New Guineans without concern for consequences, whereas New Guineans knew they would be arrested immediately and jailed for a similar assault on a European. European men sought young New Guinean women for sex, while European women were off limits to New Guinean men. Europeans had private clubs where they drank and socialized that were off limits to New Guineans. The existence of such a double standard was obvious to all, but not easily explained in palatable terms. The explanation lay in the racism evident in the vocabulary of the colonial pidgin language that applied the term *masta* to Europeans and *kanaka* and *boi* to New Guineans. That same racism underlay the European use of derogatory terms like "Rocky" (shorthand for "rock ape") in reference to New Guineans. The application of the derogatory term "gin jockey" (from Australian slang references to aboriginals) to European men who enjoyed New Guinean women as sex partners evidenced the ease with which Europeans could cross the line into the native camp. There were no comparable terms to my knowledge that designated New Guineans who had crossed to the European side of the line. Interracial relationships normally involved European men and New Guinean women. The New Guinean women were tolerated less readily by Europeans than were the men. The small number of Europeans in any particular location mandated against total exclusion of such a man. It was hoped that he might eventually "come good" and mend his ways. After all, he was a European, even if a misguided one.

This double standard was a constant source of tension for both the Imbonggu and me. I insisted that no one refer to me as Masta Bill. This was a concession to my own sensitivities about the historic roots of the term. It was not easily achieved, however, as Imbonggu were accustomed to a lifetime of such linguistic usage. Any three-way conversations involving me, an Imbi villager, and a European government officer was invariably a risky affair. The Imbi was made uncomfortable by the European's pointed use of the term *masta* to refer to me. The European was angered, even offended, by Imbi use of the overly familiar Billi or Billio or Kondoli. I found it easier in such situations to avoid confrontation by reluctantly tolerating use of *masta* and later seeking to enlighten the two other parties to the conversation in a less potentially combative situation. Even the best of intentions often find themselves thwarted by the distribution of power. The absolute ease and certainty with which the European labeled me *masta,* my modest frustration with the term, and the extreme discomfort experienced by my Imbi friend were adequate reflections of our relative status in the power structure. This experience, so often repeated, did more than any experience in America to sensitize me to the nature of institutionalized racism. That is one of my enduring debts to the Imbonggu, so many of whom were amateur anthropologists without knowing it. By looking at my own culture through their inquisitive Imbonggu eyes, I came to understand and appreciate much that I might never have observed through my culturally conditioned American eyes.

18 / Kondoli's Farewell *Moka*

Time is a very strange concept. Americans are obsessed with it. The Imbi seldom even think about it. I arrived in New Guinea with the clock ticking. I had a deadline before I began. The National Science Foundation had awarded me a doctoral dissertation research grant that would support me for two years. The Qantas pilots' strike had suspended time briefly for me, but inevitably the clock began ticking again. I initiated my fieldwork with a sense of urgency. So much to do, so little time. I needed to interview this many informants about one thing and that many informants about something else. I constructed a rough bar chart. By the end of the sixth month, I would have completed thirty migrant laborer data forms, twenty others recording disputes, a dozen more detailing brideprice negotiations and payments. I felt a very real sense of security in such organization. Time would not outrun me. I would not emerge from the tropical oven of New Guinea in some partially cooked condition.

My precise plans and schedule had taken into account every conceivable contingency except one: the Imbonggu. Migrants failed to return to the village on schedule. People wanted to talk about a great many things but not always those items I sought to discuss. Men who agreed to talk to me on Thursday would leave the village on Wednesday and remain away for a week. I began to fall behind schedule almost immediately. The Imbonggu were only partly the source of the problem. I had an opportunity to accompany Geoff Cowper on an election patrol that I had not anticipated. Simon Harrison, an anthropologist conducting contract research for the government, invited me to accompany him to the Mendi Valley for a week to record several distributions of pig meat orchestrated by Big Men. There was no hope of maintaining my schedule. I tore it up. I would observe what came my way. When the opportunity to complete one of my interview recording forms presented itself, I would take advantage of it, but I would no longer consent to being a slave to my own bar charts. It was a truly liberating experience. But cultural shackles are not easily shed. I continued to set my wristwatch daily according to the precise time ticks generated by the atomic clock in Fort Collins, Colorado. Its unerring pulse was transmitted by the American Forces Radio and Television Service to the ends of the earth, Ialibu being one according to so many of my American friends and relatives.

Time surged forward, yet somehow stood still. The months passed, but they didn't. One year turned into two, seemingly overnight. The initial excitement of arriving at Ialibu gave way to the inexplicable sense that I had always been there. The early fear that the day of my departure was rapidly approaching gave way to a vague realization that I would no doubt leave Ialibu sometime, but that departure seemed so distant it seldom intruded on my thoughts. Letters from family and friends served as occasional reminders, as did letters from the University of Pittsburgh that sought to extract any scrap of information about when I would return, how many credit hours I would enroll for, and whether or not I would be available to teach an evening class in the University's extension program. The pressure of time was beginning to reassert itself. And as Americans claim, time is money and money often buys time. Flo Moidel, my grant administrator back in Pittsburgh, sent me the final five hundred dollars available under my grant. If money buys time, I had bought all I could. For the first time since my arrival, I became obsessed with time. My fear was not with the state of my research. I would survive with what I had accomplished. I would be able to write less about some things but more about others. Rather, what caused my anxiety was the sickening realization that I would soon be somewhere else. No more stories around my hearth. No more treks through Imbonggu territory to observe feasts, divinations, weddings, funerals, arguments, or games. No more treks up the sides of Mount Ialibu for firewood, building materials, or garden produce. No more evenings of beer and darts followed by mornings and afternoons of beer and tennis.

Throughout my stay I had maintained a list of my possessions and of the individual Imbi to whom I wished to leave something at my farewell distribution. Kondoli's *moka* was no longer some vague good intention; it was next week. Some of my belongings had long been the subjects of extended debate concerning their ultimate disposition. Several women had indicated their desire to have blankets and sheets like the ones on my bed. Others had expressed intense interest in my limited supply of cooking utensils, pots, and pans. My various *gumi* (plastic containers for kerosene and chili peppers) were always highly prized. It was obvious I could not give something to each individual. My strategy was to give my material possessions to those who I owed the greatest debts of friendship and assistance. My decisions were generally accepted as correct and reasonable. One notable exception was a very good hunting knife with a leather sheath. Most items to be given away at my *moka* were little more than tangible expressions of my gratitude and affection, like locks of hair wrapped in tissue doomed to lie forgotten in a box in a closet. They were little more than keepsakes to show an Imbi grandchild not yet born, visible stimuli to fading memories. But the knife promised utility and value, and my list of *moka* recipients could not accommodate everyone. The knife, however, disappeared the day before my *moka* was set to occur. The theft of the knife had an almost debilitating effect on me. The value of the knife was far from great. I could easily replace it at a cost of a few dollars and an hour's time to visit a store a few miles away. The entire village was galvanized around the knife. A sense of communal humiliation and embarrassment set in. Streams of people came by my house to offer apologies. Men held forth in the center of the village berating the thief and demanding that the knife be returned. The next morning the knife was returned to me. More precisely, it was placed inside the door of my house during the night while I slept. Several people privately offered their own ideas about the identity of the thief. The consensus of such rumor was that the knife was stolen by the very individual to whom I had allocated it!

My *moka* went more or less according to script. With an empty house, and an empty feeling in my gut, I walked the seven kilometers from Tona to the government post for the final time. I tried to enjoy a final night of darts and beer at the Royal Ialibu Yacht Club. In the morning, Anne Cowper and I loaded my gear into her car and set off for the airport at Mount Hagen. We were joined in that final trip by Edith Elder, another member of the Ialibu expatriate community. We stopped along the road at the point where it is intersected by the walking path leading to Tona. A sea of people waited. Anne stopped the car. We were engulfed by a swell of waving and crying Imbonggu intent on hugging me one final time. The two-hour drive to the airport at Mount Hagen took an eternity as we passed landmark after landmark. Would I ever again cross the Kaugel River? Was this my last drive past Danny Leahy's coffee plantation? my last drive through the Nebilyer Valley, the valley that had given Napile her name? It was not destined to be, but I did not know it at the time. I experienced a deep depression owing to the fear that I was leaving the place I loved most on earth with the distinct possibility that I might never return.

And what lay ahead? How could I return to a city that would be covered in snow in less than three months? How would I cope with a culture that seemed committed to constantly redefining itself? Loyalty, for example. While at Ialibu I had learned of the unceremonious departure of America from Vietnam. While some Americans might be joyfully dancing in the streets of Berkeley, Vietnamese in Saigon were running down the streets of their jilted city in search of the sanctuary they hoped might save their lives. Even baseball was no longer safe from the emerging selfishness and greed of America's emerging "me generation." My beloved Minnesota Twins had committed the unthinkable while I was away. They had allowed Harmon Killebrew to play out his baseball career with the Kansas City Royals. This was serious betrayal. Several years earlier I had been forced to choose between two names for my cat. The baseball side of my brain had demanded I name him Harmon Clayton Kittybrew. The anthropology side of my brain had lobbied for Bronislaw Malinhousekitti, in honor of the anthropological legend Bronislaw Malinowski, who had beaten me to New Guinea by nearly sixty years. Baseball won, as it so often had before when I sat in the bleachers watching the Pittsburgh Pirates while I should have been in the library reading anthropology. How could I return to a society that lived and died by the clock? How could I return to a society where an individual's survival was not the shared obligation of his friends and relatives but was instead the reward for selling one's labor or skill? How could I leave a culture where accumulation of firewood was to be avoided at any cost to one where the accumulation of wealth was to be achieved at any cost? How would I cope with a society that had a law for everything and not enough courts to handle all the disputes generated by the pervasive ethic that competition is good? The Imbonggu world that lacked laws, courts, and jails and that thrived on cooperation to overcome competition seemed far preferable. But I had no alternative.

As I made that final drive from Ialibu to Mount Hagen, I sensed that I was driving through something of a metaphor. Was my return to America possibly no different than the inevitable journey of the Imbonggu from their cultural past to the cultural present of the new nation of Papua New Guinea? That nation had been created by Australia in the latter's image, which was much more like America than Imbonggu. Even if I did return to Ialibu sometime in the future, what would I find? Would people in Tona be watching syndicated reruns of *M*A*S*H* on imported Japanese television sets? Would they be dancing to zillion-watt amplifiers in the cafeteria of the local high school? Or would the Imbi have been driven away to toil in some distant plantation labor line or struggle in a squatter camp in Port Moresby? Would they be gone but not forgotten, like Harmon Killebrew?

19 / The Richest Man in America

Home is a fascinating concept. It is enshrined in cliché. Home sweet home. Home is where the heart is. Homeboy. America (Home, for Americans), love it or leave it. I can't wait to get home. There's no place like home. But like every story, home has a second side, another cliché. You can't go home again. At least you can't go home again without some sense that it isn't all that it used to be and it isn't all that it could be. As noted earlier, Peoples and Bailey warned us about anthropologists and the indigenous peoples we come to know: "We tend to identify with them, partly because of our greater familiarity with their ways of life. Also, our training usually gives us a fairly relativistic outlook on alternative ways of being human—deep immersion into other sociocultural systems leaves some of us unsure about our attachment to our own" (1988:435).

By the time I left Tona, my world had expanded to include the Imbonggu. I was frustrated and angered in my return to the United States. I merely wanted to slide back into America without being reminded daily that I must be terribly happy to be home again. Back in the land of dependable flush toilets, dependable postal service, telephones, television, and so forth. In short, a country that worked (in the sense that a clock works if it keeps time accurately) and that was populated by civilized people who wore clothes. It must surely be good to be back among Us and rid of Them, no matter how exotic They might have been for a fleeting moment of my impulsive young life. But what I came back to was a country with snow and ice rather than heat and humidity. Back to a land of high personal incomes neutralized by high taxes and high prices. And most depressing of all, back to a land where crime was commonplace.

My wife Diane and I returned to a large city. Between the time we unloaded our U-Haul into a "secure" basement and we moved everything up three flights of stairs to our apartment, we discovered the loss of two room-sized carpets, a coffee table (the thief left us with the two drawers to the table that had been set down separately from the larger piece), and our vacuum cleaner. We complained to the landlord about the obvious lack of security in his supposedly secure building. He shrugged his shoulders and speculated that the likely suspects were none other than our new downstairs neighbor and her friends. The landlord had been seeking to evict the young woman, a prostitute, for failing to pay her rent over a period of several months. Shortly after talking to the landlord, I overheard movement in the apartment below. After some inner deliberation I decided to go downstairs and confront her. By the time I reached her door she was gone, but she had left the door ajar. I called inside several times. Certain she and her friends had departed, I entered the apartment and conducted a rapid search. In one of the bedrooms our vacuum cleaner sat atop a clutter of other items.

I returned to our apartment and called the police, who arrived in rather comical fashion. We had not yet moved the bulk of our belongings from the basement to our apartment, so the police entered a bare room with nothing but a painting of a tree on one wall, the legacy of some former tenant. Responding to a report of a burglary, the police entered our nude apartment and promptly exclaimed, with both sympathy for us and admiration for the burglars, "Wow! They really got you, didn't they?" We explained that we were just moving in and that the bulk of our property was safely in other rooms and the basement and that we had lost only a few items. And best of all, I explained, we knew where they were. I related what we knew of the young lady living and working a floor beneath us. I described my cursory search of her apartment and the discovery of our vacuum cleaner. The police looked at each other and explained there was nothing they could do. They set out the requirements of the law. We would have to produce a witness who would swear to having seen the young woman or one of her friends actually move our property into her apartment. Without such a statement, no judge would issue a search warrant. Besides, they suggested delicately, I was probably guilty of breaking and entering in my unauthorized search of her apartment.

One of the police put American justice in proper perspective with one simple question, "Why didn't you just take your stuff back when you had the chance?" I was forced to admit that this was a very good question in light of these subsequent dealings with the police. Unable to take a proper report and obtain a warrant, the police set about leaving. On the way out the door, they mumbled to one another, and then turned to me. "Is she in the apartment right now?" one of them asked. No. They suggested I follow them downstairs. They stopped at the front door to the building, in clear view of her door, which was still ajar. They suggested that they had nowhere else to go for the next couple minutes, which seemed to them ample time to reclaim one small vacuum cleaner. They turned their backs to me. I took their cue and entered the apartment for the second time. I was surprised to encounter a young man to whom I explained my reason for being there. Describing himself as the young lady's former boyfriend, he admitted he was on much the same sort of mission and invited me to go about my business. So there I was, only three weeks back from a lawless and violent land, committing burglary in the company of a second burglar committing a separate one of his own. And best of all, this was all occurring in the name of justice while two armed and uniformed police officers of a major American city stood guard in the corridor. Sadly, this would not be our final brush with crime in America. Only six months later, we were forced to move to a new location when our landlord decided to convert our building to condominium units and retire to Florida to count his money. Rich Scaglion and John Frechione, good friends and anthropology colleagues, helped me load a U-Haul truck with our belongings. Finished at two in the morning and far too tired to unload the truck at our new apartment several blocks away, we went to sleep with the intention of completing the job in the morning. Six hours later, when I went to move the truck, I was sickened to discover it was no longer parked where I had left it. Fortunately, we found it only two blocks away. Frechione's father had loaned us a powerful padlock, an artifact of his days in the navy. It served us well. The thieves had been unable to break the lock. As morning light engulfed them, they simply abandoned the truck with its hot-wired engine running and its broken ignition switch lying on the floor. Yes, it was great to be back.

Homecoming was in many other ways a fascinating experience. Family and friends were indeed glad to see me. Relieved that I was home, they were decidedly uninterested in where I had been. The slides I showed with such anticipation were greeted not by enthusiastic questions betraying a desire to learn about Imbonggu life and culture and what they might offer Americans. Rather, they were greeted by moans and groans and indescribable sounds that betrayed a deep-seated fear that the Imbonggu might be somehow contagious. Merely looking at the slides seldom encouraged inquisitiveness. Instead, my slides seemed to unleash a deep-rooted cultural prejudice that manifests itself in telling questions, such as "Why don't they wear clothes?" Or observations like "They are so dirty. Don't they ever bathe?"

My efforts to explain what the Imbonggu did and why they did it were normally met with expressions of distaste and disbelief rather than admiration. "Do they really believe that magic stones kept in the roof of a house bring good luck? How silly." Months earlier, people in Tona had readily accepted the American belief that the foot of a rabbit could bring good luck. "Do they really believe that leaves can relieve muscle pain? How strange." Months before, I had explained to an audience at Ialibu how people in America believe that certain tree barks and herbs prevent some diseases and cure others. The Imbonggu understood easily enough. "Do they really believe that spirits can protect them from being injured when they walk through the forest?" The Imbonggu had little difficulty comprehending St. Christopher medals and plastic Jesus figurines on the dashboards of vehicles. What was the difference? Imbonggu kept the skulls of their dead fathers. "How awful!" squawked students in my introductory class. But what about Dad's American ashes sitting in an urn on the mantle? Spirits speaking to humans via birds or dreams apparently made no sense to members of a culture that accepts televangelists as the mouthpieces of God and visions and miracles as evidence of God's direct communication with mere mortals. Examining vomit for evidence was incomprehensible to people who accept evidence obtained by blood tests and autopsies.

But coming home meant more than merely trying to explain the Imbonggu to Americans. It meant the equally difficult but decidedly more delicate task of explaining America to Americans. "At least there is no corruption in America like there is over there." Spiro Agnew was useful at last, as an illustration, as a case study in corruption. The vice president of the United States, forced to resign over a construction kickback scandal. "It is America's responsibility to provide the model of freedom and democracy for the rest of the world." Some model. I had spent two years attempting to explain Richard Nixon, Watergate, illegal wiretapping, perjury, and cover-ups to both Imbonggu and Australians. The president of the United States, forced to resign or face being thrown out of office. One futile flashing of the victory sign before that final helicopter ride, the reward for nineteen minutes of conversation that found its way to The Twilight Zone. "At least we elect our leaders rather than having them appoint themselves." Gerald Ford, a good and decent man. And the only man ever to serve as both vice president and president of the United States without having been elected to either office. Ford was appointed to replace a disgraced vice president by a president who would himself leave office in disgrace and be replaced by the very man he had personally appointed as his unanticipated successor. It was hardly Ford's fault to wake up one morning as president of the United States. But it was hardly his good fortune in light of future events. In his only attempt to be elected president, a sort of after-the-fact quest for legitimacy, he was defeated by Jimmy Carter.

Americans lead the good life. The evidence is everywhere. I was forced to admit that no Imbonggu had ever seen a dentist. Nor a cardiologist, nor a psychiatrist. My counterarguments (that in contrast to Americans Imbonggu had few dental problems, no pattern of heart disease, and no pattern of culture-induced stress disorders leading to mental instability) were dismissed as obvious failures of observation on my part, or merely my stubborn reluctance to accept the truth. America and its citizens are wealthy. Again, the evidence is everywhere. Americans are educated, earn high incomes, have the ability to purchase the best products to satisfy their needs, are well-fed, and enjoy far more adequate housing than a thatched hut. So why do such a large number of Americans earn no money at all? Why do we have such a high rate of functional illiteracy? Why does survey after survey demonstrate that Americans are unhappy with their jobs and feel they do not earn enough money to live the way they would like? Why do so many American children go without adequate food while other Americans spend large sums of money to shed excess weight? And why have America's urban sidewalks become open-air camps providing housing that lacks the luxury of an Imbonggu thatched roof?

The Imbonggu are not at fault for American problems. And they certainly are not obligated to solve them. But Americans might learn much by examining the context of Imbonggu society and culture and isolating the factors that apparently hinder the emergence of problems like those confronting America. There is an unfortunate arrogance in the view that America is in all ways superior to everyone else. First, it is unfortunate in that the inevitable consequence is a stream of American diplomats and businesspeople invading the rest of the world with their cherished economic and moral baggage. Just as Americans dislike door-to-door salespeople, the rest of the world often finds our aggressive promotion of our products and worldview a bit repulsive. The Ugly American remains a universally held stereotype. Second, it is unfortunate in that it blinds us to the accumulated knowledge and wisdom of millennia of human experience. That experience becomes simply overwhelmed in our minds by our own short history of apparent success. One is struck by the sense of amazement that attends each scientific revelation that some tribal remedy has true medicinal value in American terms. What is most amazing is not the discovery, as if we should never have anticipated such clever applications by people like the Imbonggu, but the persistent unwillingness to look to people like the Imbonggu in the first place.

These were all frustrating and vexing problems on my return from New Guinea. I no longer saw American problems solely through American eyes. My expanded vision, however, was met not with enthusiasm but by a culturally induced blindness. I recalled a television production from my youth. I believe Lee Marvin played the lead role in "The Richest Man in Bogota." The richest man in Bogota was an immigrant with a singular gift. He was the only sighted person in a land where all the native inhabitants were blind. He possessed the ability to see what others neither could nor wished to, a potential boon to all. But a gift that reeked of sorcery to those without it. Rather than presenting the ultimate opportunity, his gift presented the ultimate dilemma. The greatest gift to one was perceived instead as the greatest threat to all. The intellectual blindness of the natives, the certainty that their way was best, proved to be more debilitating than their physical blindness. Unwilling to accept the immigrant and exploit his tremendous potential to solve their problems, the citizens of Bogota chose instead to correct what they perceived to be the immigrant's problem. He was blinded, his gift and its potential forfeited forever.

During the two years following my return from New Guinea, I reflected often on that sighted man in blind Bogota. For me, and probably most anthropologists, it is a powerful and disturbing metaphor. Who are we? What do we want to be after the rebirth experience of field research in a different culture? How do we impart the fruits of our vision to those who find comfort in the familiar fact of shared blindness? And how do we avoid becoming one of them? Of more immediate importance to me was the matter of how I, Billio, would avoid assuming the poverty of blindness that seemed too evident in the America to which I had returned.

In Ialibu I had been forced to deal with the demand that I "live like a white man." In America, an angry student evaluation form harbored the suggestion that I return to New Guinea and live like a savage if I liked it so much there. Three and one-half years after leaving Tona, I fulfilled that angry student's wish and my own. I returned to New Guinea. Those short years seemed more like eternity. What would I find in Ialibu? Equally troubling, who would I no longer find?

20 / Epilogue: Kondoli Is Back!

My second trip to Ialibu was less direct than the first. I returned to New Guinea as a Research Fellow at the Institute of Applied Social and Economic Research. When I had visited the same institute five years earlier, it had been known as the New Guinea Research Unit, a remote appendage of the Australian National University. It was an Australian gift to Papua New Guinea on the latter's political independence from the former. My primary responsibilities were to keep me in Port Moresby, a very long way from Ialibu. Papua New Guinea continues to be one of those charming but frustrating Pacific backwaters where the absence of roads combines with the vagaries of modern aviation routing and scheduling to assure that one cannot get there from here.

To my relief and frustration, Ialibu began to come to me. Several provincial administrative officials attended a development conference at the Institute shortly after my arrival. Via this budding grapevine, several past members of the Royal Ialibu Yacht Club learned of my arrival and celebrated my return with a crank telephone call placed by one of the female members. In a disguised voice, she pleaded with me to guarantee that I remember to draw my shades at night as I was driving her to distraction. Silly as this all was, it brought Ialibu one step closer. Randy Bollig, a teacher at Ialibu while I was there, now headmaster at a different high school, spent a week with me in Port Moresby while he attended a training seminar. A trip to a small artifact shop operated by the Girl Guides (the Australian designation for Girl Scouts) produced a warm reunion with Mary Wapi. Back in Ialibu, as the administrative assistant to the assistant district commissioner, Mary had aided me in navigating the file cabinets of the colonial administration. Her husband Rex, clerk to the Local Government Council, had been equally supportive. But no reunion was more exciting than mine with Victor Koiyabo.

The Boroko section of Port Moresby is one of a handful of shopping and dining areas in a city notable for the general absence of such centers. Business hours in Papua New Guinea are generally timed to coincide with working hours. Thus, if one is to shop or go to the bank during the week, one must give up working for the required time. Saturday morning is the only other time when shops are open. Consequently, Saturday morning witnesses the inundation of Boroko by a sea of jostling humanity. Many are there to shop. Others are there simply because most everyone else is. Actually, going to Boroko on a Saturday is something of an activity in its own right. Among Papua New Guineans the activity is known as *raun nating* in Neo-Melanesian. Known as "rounding" in the pidginized English of the resident foreigners, it is comparable to "hanging out" at the mall in America. One Saturday as I was wandering the congested sidewalks of Boroko, I heard a tentative

"Kondoli?" I turned to encounter Koiyabo, who had come to Port Moresby to undertake a vocational course at a local technical college. We slipped into a small restaurant, known locally as Papa Oyster's in honor of the hulking, redheaded New Zealander who operated it along with his wife and children. I gave Victor my telephone number and urged him to call me soon.

I was elated at meeting so many of my Ialibu friends in Port Moresby, but it also troubled me because three years earlier no Imbonggu lived in the city. The government of Papua New Guinea had worried for years that the rate of migration from rural areas like Ialibu to urban areas like Port Moresby was approaching dangerous levels. My research at Ialibu had led me to conclude that the fear was greatly overstated. But here in the big city there seemed to be another Imbonggu at every turn. Was the government's worst fear becoming reality? Were the Imbonggu giving up their way of life to go to town, earn money, and live in the high style represented by purple soccer shorts and orange rugby jerseys imported from China?

Victor called a few days later. He suggested we go to the races at Bomana the following Saturday. I agreed, more to see Victor than to watch the horses run. But the races were not without their own appeal. The local turf club was something of a window into the not-so-distant past, or possibly just evidence that the past was not quite past. It sported a green grandstand where the colonial gentry could watch their horses thunder clockwise around a track that must have seemed like a mined construction zone to the jockeys and their mounts. The horses were themselves interesting. Aged Australian thoroughbreds well past their prime, they were sold to purchasers in New Guinea where they would run a few more times at Bomana. A sort of fantasy camp for nags. But their aged, swaying backs supported the greatest fantasy of all: that six-foot, three-inch Australian men are to be taken seriously as jockeys. Lumbering horses, their undercarriages dragging along the track, lugged gargantuan jockeys, their feet dragging along the same abused track. A scene straight from Monty Python. And while all this was going on, Papua New Guineans crushed into a canvas-covered enclosure adjacent to the grandstand where they placed bets on horses whose names they could not pronounce and whose superior speed could only be a wild hope. This gambling was one of the many ways modern urban Papua New Guineans sought to balance their high cost of living with their low income. They even placed bets on horses they could not see. Races in Brisbane, Sydney, and Melbourne were broadcast live via radio and offered additional wagering opportunities for punters at Bomana to supplement their fortnight's earnings. Or, perhaps, simply to lose them.

Despite these rejuvenating contacts with Ialibu, my frustration deepened. I would be in Papua New Guinea for nearly eighteen months before I would make it back to Ialibu. I left the Institute after fifteen months and accepted a job in the raucous highlands frontier town of Wabag. Located in Enga Province, Wabag was one step closer to Ialibu. I began to make serious plans to return to Tona. While living in Tona before, I had made a brief trip to Enga with Randy Bollig and my wife. Diane was visiting me in the field while on a teaching break from Australia. We were very impressed with the overtly aggressive attitude of Engas, a sharp contrast to the gentle smiles that greet visitors to Ialibu. My job in Enga was to conduct extensive research into the phenomenon of tribal warfare and to assist the beleaguered government in dealing with that seemingly intractable problem. From my first day in Enga, I experienced a steady diet of death and destruction. In fairness to the Enga, I invariably caught them at their worst. I appeared on the scene to interview the relatives of recently dismembered warriors as they wallowed in their grief. On other occasions I interviewed warriors whose spirits were temporarily buoyed by the apparent joy of having recently raped, maimed, or butchered another human being. Such high spirits were invariably short-lived, however, and my informants repeatedly moved back and forth between the fraternity of elated winners and that of distraught losers. Sadly, many individual informants did not live to complete the reverse journey. Rather, their violent deaths were the cause for both the joy of the victors and the agony of the relatives of the victims. It began to appear that the Imbonggu had been right all along in their repeated admonition that the Enga would eventually kill me if I kept visiting there. Living and working among the Enga left little doubt in my mind that those warnings were not without justification. I came not only to want to return to Ialibu, I needed to. I desperately needed the smiles and good humor that could flourish only in an environment of peace.

More than five years after I left Tona, I made my first return visit. As I drove along the narrow road leading from the main highway to the administrative center of Ialibu, I found myself succumbing to doubts. Would Wakea be alive? He was so old and frail when I left. Or, at least eighty years old by this time, would his love magic have attracted yet another twenty-year-old wife? Would Peni still be in Tona, still rejecting all those brideprice offers so carefully crafted by poor Arume? Would she have given in and taken up residence in some other village? Would Mare still be in Tona, or would her name have fulfilled its promise and attracted the huge brideprice fantasized by Pera when he bestowed her name? Would I recognize anyone? I had often been struck by how rapidly Imbonggu began to show their age. It had always seemed that young girls of seventeen looked to be thirteen. Once married, after five years of working on their knees in the gardens daily and giving birth to children only slightly younger than themselves, these young women looked more like forty than twenty-five. Everyone who had reached forty years looked old and apparently continued to do so for a very long time. While I knew Imbonggu of all ages, I had not witnessed any individual Imbonggu endure the ravages of aging. With no family portrait albums, there was no record of what Yombi had looked like five years before I first arrived. I expected the adults to look much the same but feared that many of the children would be unrecognizable, having lived half of their lives since I left Tona.

Other fears centered more directly on me. Would anyone recognize me? They would certainly detect a noticeable weight gain. Ironically, something viewed with such negativity by Americans would almost certainly be greeted by the Imbonggu with a sense of relief in the knowledge that my health had not failed. As the rigors of bush living and changing diet had shrunk me on my first trip to Tona, women had repeatedly observed that I must be ill. My obvious return to good health would not go unnoticed. Would people welcome me to live in the village again? What about the few people I knew I had antagonized? Would they harbor a grudge? Would I learn anything about the fates of Bis and Brus (Beast and Brute, those two Siamese beauties forced to survive in a world of mangy mutts)? Kani had once written that the two cats had disappeared. She suspected that they had been captured and eaten. I left Tona hoping that their obvious abilities as hunters and their demonstrated utility in ridding houses of rats would provide the two cats a mantle of privilege. Kani predicted they would more likely become *bilas* (decoration).

Tona came into view around a turn in the narrow road. I saw a small child running away at breakneck speed. Some things had not changed. When I pulled my small Suzuki jeep look-alike off the road, a handful of children stood looking at me from atop a small pile of earth nearby. None looked old enough to have been born while I was in Tona before. A glance over the hill and down the path to the village revealed people running in every direction and yelling "Billio" and "Kondoli" and gesturing in my general direction. People came running from everywhere. Turumbu and Puiya, now practicing Catholics named Steven and Priscilla, were among the first to reach me. Purul, formerly a short and gaunt boy of thirteen, now looked down at me from his majestic height of slightly over six feet. In only five years I had surrendered my title as tallest person in Tona to a mere child. As we walked down the path to the village, the crowd of children continued to grow. Here and there I recognized one, most were new to me.

As we entered the village proper, the most visible symbol of change stared at me from the opposite end of the dance ground. There was now a *haus lotu* (church, literally "house Lord") in Tona. People still trekked the seven miles to the Capuchin mission to attend Sunday services, but evening Bible study was conducted in Tona by village leaders in the Catholic church. The new church also provided the venue for what might best be described as hymn-alongs. Christian hymns had replaced the

Back in Tona with Imbi children

twangy melodies of Australian vocalists like Slim Dusty. The Boy from Alabama and the Girl from Gundagai had deferred to an equally foreign Holy Father and Blessed Virgin.

Displaying their customary reserve, the adults had not raced frantically to greet me at the road. They had waited patiently in Tona, sitting on the grass. Yombi was positively dapper for the occasion in his blue sport jacket, *bilum,* and kina shell. Puiya looked more like her mother than her self of five years earlier. Alerapu had grown to an impressive height, particularly for a woman, and this eighteen-year-old was now taller than her sister Peni had been at the same age. Arume, as always, sat quietly on the margin neither in nor out of the flow of events. As I remembered him, he was merely there, the timid byproduct of years of fruitless attempts to arrange Peni's marriage. In my mind I could hear him musing to himself whether this was the time. Was I finally the one? We talked later. Peni was no longer in Tona. She had married a teacher and was living in Goroka.

After the obligatory tour of the village, including a visit to the *haus lotu,* I joined Yombi and the others on the grass before his house. To the rear of his house was a large sugar cane plot gracing the spot where my house had stood and ultimately fallen into disrepair. "We can rebuild there if you like," offered Yombi. While we talked, several young men busied themselves playing at their homemade version of pool. They used *pitpit* cues to direct glass marbles through openings at the corners of a makeshift miniature pool table propped atop an empty metal drum, like some open-air variety of the Royal Ialibu Yacht Club. Nonge suggested that we take some reunion photographs. I became the stock backdrop for a seemingly endless series of substitutions as men sat before the camera and then relinquished their spots to others for more photographs.

These formalities of greeting out of the way, we launched into far more substantial conversation. Much of it gave me the sense that, like Rip van Winkle, I might have missed much more in my absence than I initially thought. Five years earlier, men had asked me repeatedly to explain how political parties worked and what the national parliamentary election was all about. Now I was treated to a recitation of very sophisticated analyses of the platforms of the Pangu Party and the People's Progress Party, as well as the performance of various elected officials. Yombi noted that as poor as the people of Tona had been six years ago, it was far worse now. After all, he observed, inflation had become a major problem. He actually used the word! He offhandedly noted that it would cost much more to rebuild my house than it had originally, barely eight years earlier. Politics? Inflation? These were some of the same reasons I had become so disappointed with life in America. Was there no escape?

After this initial wave of shock had washed over me, it was agreed that Steven and Priscilla would join Diane and me in a drive to Mendi the next day. We would attempt to make contact with Mare. She was now married to a Mendi man and living about thirty miles from Tona. Steven and I discussed the building of a house for me in Tona. I had always enjoyed a spot overlooking the small stream that had failed to relieve the discomfort of Yala and the others who had eaten my chili peppers. Steven's father, Yunungo, controlled the site. He agreed that I could build a house on it. Steven would do the construction. Trained as a carpenter at a Catholic vocational school in Tari, he was excited at the prospect of applying his skills. We agreed on a budget, and I gave him some cash as an advance to purchase necessary tools and materials. Steven expressed a desire for an additional reward on completion of the house—a wristwatch.

One of the primary reasons I had longed to return to Tona was the sense of timelessness I had experienced there. But here I was, paying for the construction of my new house with money and a wristwatch. Time had come to the timeless. This amazing irony, like so many incongruities I had found so fascinating about the Imbonggu, released waves of emotions. I had left Tona one morning nearly six years earlier. I had taken with me a picture of the Imbi. That photograph, imprinted in my mind, had frozen them in time. But were the Imbi of that photo and the Imbi of this day the same? There was reason to doubt. I had listened to Yombi discuss inflation and Wakea analyze recent political events. I had watched Purul play billiards with *pitpit* and marbles against a backdrop that included a new *haus lotu*. And Peni and Mare, no longer living in Tona, had disappeared from the photo entirely. Mount Giluwe and Mount Ialibu remained unchanged, however, as if to provide undeniable evidence that I was in the right place.

I began to experience conflicting emotions. It was great to be back in Tona. But it was a different Tona. Much had changed in five years, but those changes provided opportunities for new photographs and new fieldnotes that would inform my continuing effort to understand the Imbonggu. It struck me that I had experienced similar uncertainty years before when I first came to Ialibu. I experienced similar anxieties again when I left Ialibu and returned to America more than two years later. And here I was one more time. In the immortal words of Yogi Berra, "It's *deja vu* all over again!" Yogi insists he never said it. I wish he had. I know what he would have meant.

Glossary of Key Words

balus: airplane
bikhet: arrogant; overly confident
bilas: decoration
bilum: a woven string bag used by women to carry loads
boi: New Guinean laborer or servant
dimdim: slang term applied to Europeans by New Guineans
grisim: to flatter, to cajole, to bribe
gumi: plastic or rubber container; inflatable inner tube
haus lotu: church
hausboi: male domestic servant
hausmeri: female domestic servant
kanaka: unflattering label for unsophisticated New Guineans
kina: shells worn around the neck, exchanged as valuables; national minted currency of Papua New Guinea
kondodl: the color red (in Imbonggu)
kunai: a grass common to the highlands region
kuru: a neurological disease among the Fore people
laplap: imported cloth normally worn as a wrap by women
longlong: insane; deranged
masta: common term used by New Guineans to refer to Europeans
moka: a ceremonial exchange system
muruk: brand of tobacco; cassowary
oli: slang term applied to New Guineans by Europeans
pekpek: excreta
pitpit: a grass; much like bamboo, but smaller diameter
raun nating: to wander around, doing nothing in particular
tanimtok: translator
toea: minted currency of Papua New Guinea (100 equal one kina)
tumbuna: ancestors
Wok Meri: a business cooperative established and operated by women in the Daulo region of the Eastern Highlands Province
wokabaut: to walk, hike, trek

References Cited

Arens, William

1979 *The Man-eating Myth: Anthropology and Anthropophagy*. New York: Oxford University Press.

Blong, Russell J.

1982 *The Time of Darkness: Local Legend and Volcanic Reality in Papua New Guinea*. Canberra: Australian National University Press.

Champion, Ivan F.

1932 *Across New Guinea from the Fly to the Sepik*. London: Constable.

Connolly, Bob, and Robin Anderson

1983 *First Contact* (film). Sydney: Australian Broadcasting Commission.

1987 *First Contact: New Guinea's Highlanders Encounter the Outside World*. New York: Penguin Books.

Deloria, Vine

1969 *Custer Died for Your Sins*. New York: Avon Books.

Dower, John W.

1986 *War Without Mercy: Race and Power in the Pacific War*. New York: Pantheon Books.

Golson, Jack

1982 The Ipomoean Revolution Revisited: Society and the Sweet Potato in the Upper Wahgi Valley. In *Inequality in New Guinea Highlands Societies,* Andrew Strathern, ed. Pp. 109–136. Cambridge: Cambridge University Press.

Good, Kenneth

1991 *Into the Heart: One Man's Pursuit of Love and Knowledge Among the Yanomama*. New York: Simon and Schuster.

Granada Television International

1974 *The Kawelka: Ongka's Big Moka*. A film in the Disappearing Worlds series. Anthropologist: Andrew Strathern. 52 min.

Herdt, Gilbert

1987 *The Sambia: Ritual and Gender in New Guinea*. New York: Holt, Rinehart and Winston.

Hides, Jack

1935 *Through Wildest Papua*. London: Blackie and Son.

Hogbin, Ian

1970 *The Island of Menstruating Men: Religion in Wogeo, New Guinea*. Scranton: Chandler Publishing Company.

Josephides, Lisette

1985 *The Production of Inequality*. London: Tavistock.

Langness, Lewis

1967 Sexual Antagonism in the New Guinea Highlands: A Bena Bena Example. *Oceania* 37:161-177.

Leahy, Michael J.

1991 *Explorations into Highland New Guinea, 1930–1935*. Douglas E. Jones, ed. Tuscaloosa: The University of Alabama Press.

Lederman, Rena
1986 *What Gifts Engender: Social Relations and Politics in Mendi, Highland Papua New Guinea*. Cambridge: Cambridge University Press.
Malinowski, Bronislaw
1922 *Argonauts of the Western Pacific*. New York: E.P. Dutton and Company, Inc.
1967 *A Diary in the Strict Sense of the Term*. New York: Harcourt, Brace and World, Inc.
Meggitt, Mervyn
1964 Male-Female Relationships in the Highlands of Australian New Guinea. In *New Guinea: The Central Highlands. American Anthropologist* 66 (part 2):204–224.
Peoples, James, and Garrick Bailey
1988 *Humanity, An Introduction to Cultural Anthropology*. St. Paul: West Publishing Company.
Rabinow, Paul
1977 *Reflections on Fieldwork in Morocco*. Berkeley: University of California Press.
Sahlins, Marshall
1963 Poor Man, Rich Man, Big Man, Chief. *Comparative Studies in Society and History* 5:205–213.
Schieffelin, Edward L.
1976 *The Sorrow of the Lonely and the Burning of the Dancers*. New York: St. Martin's Press.
Schieffelin, Edward L., and Robert Crittenden, eds.
1991 *Like People You See in a Dream: First Contact in Six Papuan Societies*. Stanford: Stanford University Press.
Sexton, Lorraine
1986 *Mothers of Money, Daughters of Coffee: The* Wok Meri *Movement*. Ann Arbor: UMI Research Press.
Sinclair, James
1966 *Behind the Ranges: Patrolling in New Guinea*. Melbourne: Melbourne University Press.
Stocking, George W., Jr., ed.
1983 The Ethnographer's Magic: Fieldwork in British Anthropology from Tylor to Malinowski. In *Observers Observed,* G. Stocking, ed. *History of Anthropology* 1:70–120.
Strathern, Andrew
1971 *Rope of Moka: Big Men and Ceremonial Exchange in Mount Hagen*. Cambridge: Cambridge University Press.
Strathern, Marilyn
1972 *Women in Between: Female Roles in a Male World, Mount Hagen, New Guinea.* London: Seminar Press.
Whitehead, Tony Larry, and Mary Ellen Conaway, eds.
1986 *Self, Sex and Gender in Cross-Cultural Fieldwork*. Champaign: University of Illinois Press.
Wormsley, William E.
1978 Imbonggu Culture and Change: Traditional Society, Labor Migration, and Change in the Southern Highlands Province, Papua New Guinea. Ph.D. dissertation, University Microfilms International, Ann Arbor.
1981 Tradition and Change in Imbonggu Names and Naming Practices. *Names* 28:183–194.